Higher Education, Social Class and Social Mobility

Ann-Marie Bathmaker • Nicola Ingram • Jessie Abrahams
• Anthony Hoare • Richard Waller • Harriet Bradley

Higher Education, Social Class and Social Mobility

The Degree Generation

Ann-Marie Bathmaker
School of Education, University of
Birmingham, Birmingham, UK

Nicola Ingram
Educational Research, Lancaster
University, Lancaster, UK

Jessie Abrahams
School of Social Sciences, Cardiff
University, Cardiff, UK

Anthony Hoare
School of Geographical Sciences
University of Bristol, Bristol, UK

Richard Waller
School of Education (S Block)
University of the West of England
Bristol, UK

Harriet Bradley
Faculty of Business and Law
University of the West of England
Bristol, UK

Higher Education, Social Class and Social Mobility
ISBN 978-1-137-53480-4   ISBN 978-1-137-53481-1   (eBook)
DOI 10.1057/978-1-137-53481-1

Library of Congress Control Number: 2016945988

Cover image © antoni halim / Alamy Stock Photo

Printed on acid-free paper

This Palgrave Macmillan imprint is published by Springer Nature
The registered company is Macmillan Publishers Ltd. London

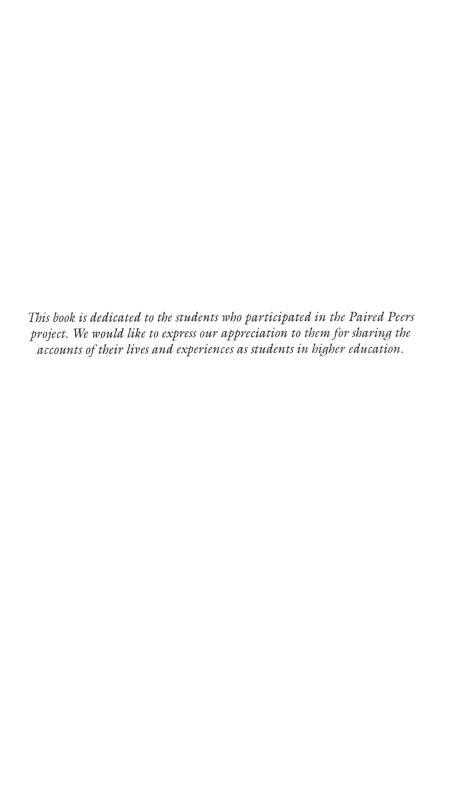

This book is dedicated to the students who participated in the Paired Peers project. We would like to express our appreciation to them for sharing the accounts of their lives and experiences as students in higher education.

FOREWORD

THE DEGREE GENERATION: HIGHER EDUCATION, SOCIAL CLASS AND SOCIAL MOBILITY

The study of social inequalities and social mobility is back on the political agenda. Following the financial crisis of 2008 and the resulting Great Recession, there has been growing public concern about the unequal distribution of income and wealth. Reports of bankers continuing to pay themselves large bonuses despite their role in the financial crisis, while other workers were losing their jobs or experiencing pay cuts, have raised issues about the kinds of people who are appointed to elite jobs as well as the way we reward them. It has also led to growing concerns about whether Britain is creating a new 'aristocracy of talent' making it even more difficult for students from working-class backgrounds to be recognized as 'high-potential' employees despite gaining access to university education. This seems a far cry from the rhetoric of the knowledge-driven economy in the decade prior to the Great Recession, when it was assumed that globalization and new technologies would increase the demand for people in high-level professional and managerial jobs. The expansion of higher education was also seen to reflect this demand, following an evolutionary path towards a fairer and more meritocratic society.

This book makes a major contribution to these debates because it offers important insights into the role of higher education in the (re)production of social inequalities. It is particularly timely because higher education has moved from being of marginal political and public policy interest to being seen as offering the best way of addressing social inequalities and increasing social mobility.

When we published *Higher Education and Corporate Realities* (1994) we wanted to draw attention to the social class consequences of an expanding system of higher education at a time when companies were shifting their hiring policies, by restructuring operations in response to a rising supply of graduate labour. *The Degree Generation* takes this study as a starting point to examine the similarities and differences in social class access, opportunities and experiences in higher education. There is no doubt that the further expansion of higher education and changes in funding arrangements, and in the employment prospects of graduates, have transformed the social and economic landscape. According to the Office for National Statistics almost half of the graduates in 2013 were underemployed. Therefore, it could be argued that the focus on social class matters even more than when we conducted our initial study. If there are more people with a bachelor's degree and a lack of decent jobs, the question of who gets a positional advantage in higher education and how this shapes labour market opportunities really matters.

To understand how social class shapes the structures and experiences of higher education the authors adopted an innovative research design. It emerged from a common initiative launched by the University of Bristol (UoB) and the University of the West of England (UWE). The UoB is located in an upmarket part of the city and is a member of the elite Russell Group of British/UK universities. UWE has a number of campuses with most of its students located on the outskirts of the city. It brands itself as 'The University of the Real World', but even so only 29% of its students are from working-class backgrounds. In response to concerns about the relatively low proportion of students from less-privileged backgrounds, both universities have attempted various initiatives to widen participation. This led to what became known as the *Paired Peers* project where students starting out at the two universities were matched by class background and subject of study. A major strength of this research design is that it enabled direct comparison of how students experienced their higher education beyond the lecture theatre. Another major strength is that students were followed throughout their time at university. Most of those interviewed maintained an interest in the project with many of them being interviewed six times over a three-year period. The quality of data generated by this study was brought home to me when I participated in a major dissemination event at the end of the project. In most of our research, those we interview remain largely invisible despite the fact that the quality of our 'findings' depends on the willingness of respondents to share their experiences. It was therefore refreshing to listen to students from different backgrounds and from the two universities sharing a platform at this event. For me the students were the 'stars of the show' and it helps to explain why this is an especially valuable study.

As a result of this approach the authors are able to present a contextually rich and interesting account of what university means to these students and how their experiences are shaped by social class inequalities, which are often intangible yet have a powerful influence on university life. The imposition of class inequalities is played out not only in obvious differences in which halls of residence the students can afford to live, but also in club membership, chatty references to overseas travel, skiing holidays and gastro dining. The focus on class is developed through insights into how gender, race and ethnicity related to patterns of social advantage and disadvantage.

In some respects there is considerable continuity with our study in the 1990s, but what this research captures, is the changing experiences of those designated as 'middle class'. It tells a story of how parents from middle-class backgrounds are being forced to mobilize more of their resources because their offspring have to run faster to stand still. Simply coming from a middle-class background is no longer enough to develop the 'cultural capital' required for success in education and the labour market. The authors show that at the same time that those from less-advantaged backgrounds may feel like 'fish out of water' in elite universities, some middle-class students may also feel like fish out of water in less-prestigious universities. This does not make it any easier for those from working-class backgrounds to compete as the bar has been raised for everyone. It is those with the money, networks and cultural resources who are most able to stay in the competition and find ways of sustaining their privileged class location.

The book challenges, in my view correctly, much of today's policy rhetoric of widening access and social mobility. It seems that we have entered a world of fantasy rhetoric as the Conservative government endorses social mobility as a policy objective at the same time as cutting support grants for the least privileged students. Their policies are also reinforcing the hierarchical ranking of Britain's universities that ultimately benefit those

x FOREWORD

with the deepest pockets to win for their children a competitive advantage in entry to elite institutions.

Perhaps, not surprisingly, the education system is identified as part of the problem, but at the same time it has an important role to play in making Britain a fairer, more tolerant and inclusive society. Here I was struck by a quotation from Henry in the concluding chapter. He comes from a working-class background and described his university experiences at UWE as surpassing his expectations, 'it's been absolutely brilliant, time of my life sort of thing'. For me this raised an intriguing question. Henry may not improve his relative chances of occupational success in competition with UoB students with similar grades but going to university has still had an impact on his sense of self, which should not be overlooked. Yet the question is whether the social confidence that some students from working-class backgrounds gain at university can be maintained in a labour market context, where it is difficult to find what used to be called a 'graduate' job—not to be confused with the idea that a graduate job is simply 'jobs that graduates do'. The good news is that this book can be read as Part I of an ongoing story, because the research team is now following some of these students into the labour market. We will have to wait for the next book, but what is presented in *The Degree Generation* deserves to be widely read and debated.

Phil Brown   Cardiff University
Distinguished Research Professor   Cardiff, UK

Acknowledgements

This book is based on the *Paired Peers* project, which was funded by the Leverhulme Trust (2010–2013). We thank the Leverhulme Trust, whose funding enabled us to undertake the study.

The Higher Education Funding Council for England provided support for the project and helped to fund dissemination events. We are grateful to them and in particular to Richard Smith and John Selby, who worked with us over the duration of the project.

We also received financial support from UWE Bristol and the University of Bristol for the final dissemination event held in London in 2013, and we thank the two universities and their vice chancellors for their contribution.

We extend our thanks to the advisory group for the project: Phil Brown, Geoff Channon, Gill Crozier, Julie McLeod, Kate Purcell, Diane Reay, Susan Robertson, John Selby and Richard Smith. They provided helpful and constructive ideas, feedback and critical insights throughout.

The members of the research team for the *Paired Peers* project were Jessie Abrahams, Ann-Marie Bathmaker, Phoebe Beedell, Harriet Bradley, Tony Hoare, Nicola Ingram, Jody Mellor and Richard Waller. Phoebe Beedell and Jody Mellor moved on to other work and projects before the writing of this book, and we thank them for their contribution to the research on which the book is based. We were assisted in the statistical work for the project by Louis Devenish and Neil Harrison and express our appreciation for their help.

We also thank Palgrave Macmillan, and Andrew James and Eleanor Christie in particular, for commissioning the book and supporting us during its production.

Finally we record our thanks to the two universities in Bristol, UWE Bristol and the University of Bristol, for their willingness to allow us to undertake this research, and also the eleven departments in the two universities who gave us access to their students and whose experience form the basis for this book. Our book is dedicated to those students.

CONTENTS

About the Authors

Jessie Abrahams is a post-doctoral research fellow at the University of Surrey on the European Research Council EuroStudents project. She was an ESRC PhD scholarship winner, and completed her PhD at Cardiff University in the School of Social Sciences. Her doctoral research focussed on class inequality in the contemporary English education system, with a specific focus on how schools reproduce inequality through their practices. She is particularly interested in the work of Pierre Bourdieu and is a co-convenor of the British Sociological Association (BSA) Bourdieu Study Group.

Ann-Marie Bathmaker is Professor of Vocational and Higher Education at the University of Birmingham. Her research focuses on questions of equity and inequalities in vocational, post-compulsory and higher education. She has a particular interest in the role of further education colleges and their international equivalents in the provision of education and training, including higher level vocational education, and she has published widely in these areas. She has recently acted as a specialist advisor to a UK Select Committee investigating school to work transitions and social mobility.

Harriet Bradley is Professor of Women's Employment at UWE Bristol and a member of the Centre for Employment Studies Research. Her research interests encompass social inequalities, work and employment and trade union studies. Her most recent publications are updated editions of her books *Gender* and *Fractured Identities*.

Dr Anthony Hoare is an Honorary member of staff of the University of Bristol's Student Recruitment, Access and Admissions Department, having been the University's inaugural Director of Research in Widening Participation between 2006 and 2015, when he took retirement. Prior to that, he was an academic member of staff in the School of Geographical Sciences at the same University, having also worked in the departments of Queen's, Belfast, The University of Canterbury (Christchurch, New Zealand) and York University, Toronto. His undergraduate and PhD degrees in Geography are from the University of Cambridge. One of his academic research interests is into the structure and spatial organization of the UK higher education sector, where he has published a number of papers and held a range of University administrative and committee positions. As Director of Widening Participation (WP) research at Bristol he undertook directly, and promoted, a range of research projects by other university colleagues, to support the University's WP policies and practices through empirical evidence. He has worked as HE consultant and commissioned researcher to the UK's major stakeholder groups and made presentations to them, at national conferences and through conferences and invited seminars. He was the inaugural chair of the Bristol/UWE joint research committee on WP and was the initial promoter of the proposal that became the *Paired Peers* projects.

Nicola Ingram is Lecturer in Education and Social Justice at Lancaster University. Her research interests are in social class inequalities in education. She is particularly interested in identity issues associated with social mobility and educational success. Nicola is co-founder of the BSA Bourdieu Study Group and has recently co-edited *Bourdieu—The Next Generation: The Development of Bourdieu's Intellectual Heritage in Contemporary UK Sociology*.

Dr Richard Waller is Associate Professor of the Sociology of Education at University of the West of England, Bristol. He has taught in further and higher education for over 20 years and published widely on issues relating to those sectors. His research interests include post-compulsory education; social justice; identity; risk; social class; masculinity; qualitative research methods; student experience and financing of higher education. He is on the editorial boards of four academic journals and is currently working on three other books for publication in 2016 or 2017.

ABBREVIATIONS

A Level	Advanced Level
BAME	Black, Asian and Minority Ethnic
BBC	British Broadcasting Corporation
BIS	(Department of) Business, Innovation and Skills
DeLHE	Destination of Leavers from Higher Education
ECA	Extra-curricular Activities
ESRC	Economic and Social Research Council
FCA	Financial Conduct Authority
FTSE (index)	Financial Times Stock Exchange (index)
GCSE	General Certificate of Secondary Education
HE	Higher Education
HEI	Higher Education Institution
HEFCE	Higher Education Funding Council for England
HESA	Higher Education Statistical Authority
LPC	Legal Practice Course
MOOC	Massive Open Online Course
NS-SEC	National Statistics Socio-Economic Classification
OFFA	Office for Fair Access
PGCE	Postgraduate Certificate in Education
REF	Research Excellence Framework
TEF	Teaching Excellence Framework
UoB	University of Bristol
UCAS	Universities and Colleges Admissions Service
UCL	University College, London
UWE	University of the West of England
UWIC	University of Wales Institute, Cardiff
WP	Widening Participation

LIST OF FIGURES

LIST OF TABLES

CHAPTER 1

The Degree Generation: Higher Education and Social Class

> Our core purpose is advancing knowledge, inspiring people, transforming futures.
>
> (2020 Plan, UWE Bristol)
>
> Our mission: to pursue and share knowledge and understanding, both for their own sake and to help individuals and society fulfil their potential.
>
> (Vision and Strategy 2009–2016, University of Bristol)

Higher education (HE) has been much in the news in the past decades. For individuals, it is currently seen as a means of developing a career and getting secure employment. Traditionally, for many young people, especially those from middle-class backgrounds, it has been an enjoyable way to bridge the transition from youth to adulthood; Brake (1980) has used the word 'moratorium' to describe this phase, which allows young people to explore and experiment with their identities free from the responsibilities of wage-earning. By society it is currently viewed as a means of identifying and fostering talent to fill professional roles and also as a means of promoting social mobility; in addition, HE professionals are likely to cling to an older vision, where universities have a key humanist mission in equipping individuals and society with the tools of rationality and enlightenment (see for example Docherty 2011; Inglis 2004; Evans 2005), and this transformative agenda seems to be reflected in the mission statements from the University of the West of England (UWE Bristol) and the University of Bristol (UoB) quoted above. Increasingly, parents believe that their

© The Editor(s) (if applicable) and The Author(s) 2016
A.M. Bathmaker et al., *Higher Education, Social Class and Social Mobility*, DOI 10.1057/978-1-137-53481-1_1

children need a university education to get on in life, and middle-class parents over the past decades have become fearful that without a degree their children will be in danger of downward social mobility (Lareau 2003; Devine 2004). Though working-class parents may not have participated in HE themselves, there is evidence that they, too, see a degree as desirable and hope that their children will continue to HE (Bradley 2015).

In the UK, where our study is located, a university degree has, at least up to the present, been a sound investment. There is a clear 'graduate premium' in earnings, which applies especially for women, compared to their non-graduate counterparts (though women continue to earn on average 23 % less than men). Recent analysis by Britton et al. (2015) using a range of datasets (UK government administrative data and Labour Force Survey data) shows that 10 years after graduation women earn three times as much as non-graduate women, while graduate men's earnings are twice that of non-graduate men. Moreover analysis of the Destination of Leavers from Higher Education (DeLHE) data by the Higher Education Statistics Agency (HESA 2015) shows that unemployment is lower amongst graduates, running at 8 % six months after graduation and 3 % after three years and six months, although there has been a recent increase in graduates working part-time. As Shamus Rahman Khan puts it in his study of elite schooling in America, 'One of the best predictors of your earnings is your level of education; attending an elite educational institution increases your wages even further. Schooling matters for wealth' (Khan 2012, p. 7).

Politically, HE can be viewed as an instrument of social justice, or conversely as a tool for elite reproduction. Over the past decades the proportion of children from working-class families attending university has been steadily if slowly increasing, in line with the target set by the UK's New Labour government (1997–2010) for 50 % of young people to participate in some form of HE by the age of 30. Dorling's (2015) analysis of recent admissions data (UCAS 2014), which was published in the *Times Higher Education* in February 2015, discusses this trend. The data show that between 2009 and 2014 the percentage of English school-leavers who entered university, who were eligible for free school meals (the key proxy for disadvantaged socio-economic background in schools), had risen from 10 to 15 %. Dorling attributes this to their improved performance in GCSE at 16. The proportion of pupils eligible for free school meals gaining five good grades (A* to C) rose dramatically between 2005 and 2013 from 18 to 38 %, highlighted as one of the few great recent successes for mobility by the Social Mobility and Child Poverty Commission (2014).

This positive trend in HE participation has manifested despite the transfer of the cost of tuition fees to individuals, first introduced by the Labour government in 1998, capped at £3000 by Labour in 2004, and then increased to a maximum of £9000 under the Conservative and Liberal Democrat Coalition government in 2012. Large demonstrations by angry young people, including school students, shocked the nation into awareness of these issues during the initial years of the Coalition government. In the year after the imposition of fees, applications did fall, but they have returned to pre-£9000 fee levels, although there has been a decline in applications from part-time and mature students, who often originate from working-class communities. In addition, the cap on the number of students that a HE institution can admit has been raised, and the level of acceptances has increased more sharply still. As Dorling points out, this is due to the actions of universities who are keen to amass more fees, and who have subsequently heightened their marketing and outreach activities.

A further trend has been an increase in students from disadvantaged backgrounds being accepted into 'elite' universities with the highest tariff entrance requirements (in terms of Advanced Level grades). UCAS, the UK's higher education admissions service, calculated that there had been a 40 % rise in students from the least advantaged areas gaining entry to elite universities between 2011 and 2014 (UCAS 2014). Although this appears on the face of it impressive, Dorling points out that this rise was from an extremely low base, constituting an increase from only 2.3 to 3.2 % of children from the poorest parts of the UK attending the most prestigious universities. They are seven times less likely to do so than their peers from advantaged backgrounds. In some parliamentary constituencies only one in seven, and sometimes only one in ten young people progressed to HE of any kind in 2014. These constituencies include Bristol East and Bristol South, the more disadvantaged areas of the city where our research study was based.

Policy debates have continued to rage about the imposition of increasing levels of fees and the safeguarding of access for the less privileged by means of bursaries. Although the existence of bursaries may have helped to ensure that the trend of working-class participation in HE has not as yet gone into reverse, it should be remembered that tuition fees are only one part of the costs of university. Students must also find funding for accommodation and living costs, which is likely to increase the level of debt with which poorer students are burdened upon finishing their studies.

If, subsequently, they find themselves unable to find the well-paid jobs they hoped for, a general climate of disillusionment may develop, with adverse effects on future student recruitment. One of the earliest acts of the UK Conservative Government elected in May 2015 was to abolish the maintenance grants which were available to students from poor backgrounds, to be replaced by further loans. This means that such students, whose families are unable to help them with the costs of food, travel and accommodation, will leave university with an even higher level of debt than the £27,000 or £36,000 incurred for the payment of fees for their three or four years of undergraduate study.

Since the establishment of the new fees regime and imposition of market values in the HE sector, universities themselves have become fixated on the 'student experience', since parents and students increasingly demand value for money, given the extent of their investment and the burden of debt students carry. This has subtly altered the relations between lecturers and their students, who have been reconstructed in the vocabulary of HE as 'customers'. As we shall see in subsequent chapters, student behaviour may change if they feel they are not getting their 'money's worth'. Former Vice-Chancellor, Peter Scott, now professor of higher education studies, has argued that the obsession with the student experience is a worrying sign of the commodification of education. Instead of investing in academic staff, universities are increasingly pouring money into new buildings and facilities that they think will attract more students:

> Universities, jittery about how they will score in the national student survey, have invested in iconic new student centres, airy atria containing banks of mac [computers] (ideally). They offer more and more 'customer services'. They do 'feedback' to death. (Scott 2015)

Scott suggests that this fixation on such a manufactured type of 'experience' may actually stifle the initiative, creativity and independence of students, and that the integrity of education may be challenged when 'student satisfaction' becomes the arbiter rather than intellectual rigour. This trend may be heightened by the Teaching Excellence Framework (TEF), heralded in the 2015 Green Paper on higher education, which will seek to assess teaching and learning performance of universities via standardized measures, such as scores in the National Student Survey or data on student destinations (BIS 2015).

Behind all these debates lies the 'elephant in the room': the reality of the impact of class which affects every aspect of people's lives and is inextricably implicated in the workings of the English education system, which can be seen as more or less stratified along class lines. The affluent classes ('dominant' classes in the terminology of Pierre Bourdieu) send their children to independent private schools, including the historic and ironically named 'public schools' such as Eton, Harrow and Rugby. The middle-classes manipulate the housing market and take up church attendance to get their children into the best primary schools (often 'church schools') and the higher-rated state schools and grammars. Working-class people usually have little choice (despite all the political rhetoric of 'parental choice') but to send their children to local state comprehensives, often derogatively referred to as 'bog standard', a term first used by Labour's Alistair Campbell in 2001 (Clare and Jones 2001; Northen 2011). The school you attend has a considerable impact on your career opportunities, influencing whether you go on to HE and what type of university you attend. There is a clear status hierarchy amongst the universities, and independent schools are adept at playing the system and getting their pupils into the highest-rated institutions, especially Oxford and Cambridge. This, after all, is why parents are happy to pay the considerable fees charged by these schools.

This book is a study of how those most intimately involved in this nexus of privilege and disadvantage, the undergraduate students, experience the HE system and how that experience is shaped by their class background. It follows the fortunes of a cohort of students at two contrasting universities. How did they get there? What did they do during their years of study? What opportunities, and what problems and obstacles did they encounter, and how did they progress? And at the end of their undergraduate studies, where were they headed and how had their career aspirations evolved? The rest of this chapter looks briefly at the sociological and policy contexts in which the research study *Paired Peers* was carried out and introduces the reader to the objectives, methods and perspectives of the research.

CLASS, EDUCATION AND POLICY

In the early 1990s, Brown and Scase carried out a study of class differences in the experiences of university students, carrying out interviews in three different types of university, that they named Oxbridge, Home Counties (a product of the postwar expansion) and Inner City (a post-1992 university).

It was published as *Higher Education and Corporate Realities* (1994). The research was conducted at a crucial moment when polytechnics in the UK were being transformed into universities in an attempt to break down the distinction by which, as one lecturer stated, 'polytechnics are the poor man's universities' (1994, p. 81). This was a world in which working-class people were still seen as a rarity in elite universities. They were, in the title of a much later study of class in HE, 'Strangers in Paradise' (Reay et al. 2009). The gender balance in the 1990s was different too. Women constituted 40 % of the undergraduate body, whereas now they are over 50 % in many subject areas, including those linked to the elite professions of law and medicine.

Brown and Scase were interested in the job opportunities which faced these undergraduates, arguing that the economy was going through a transformation. They distinguished a shift from bureaucratic organizations to what they termed 'adaptive' or 'flexible' organizations. These in turn required a new type of senior employee, whom they identified as having a 'charismatic' as opposed to 'bureaucratic' personality. This meant that recruiters were looking beyond technical skills to evidence of initiative and individuality. They were beginning to change their techniques from relying on curriculum vitae (CV) and interview. The first assessment centres were being set up; companies were looking for people who had captained sports teams or 'rowed up the Amazon in a canoe'. Brown and Scase argued that this would disadvantage poorer working-class students who lacked the resources to take part in these activities.

Since Brown and Scase carried out their study, the world has moved on but much has stayed the same. The trend to recruitment practices focused on personality as much as qualifications was only just taking off in the 1990s, but now most graduate employers put their potential recruits through an array of tests and activities, which go well beyond the former standard interview process. Applying for places on graduate schemes has become a laborious, time-consuming and daunting process, as we shall see in Chapter 6.

The university sector has also evolved considerably. The granting of university status to the former polytechnics as a result of the 1992 Further and Higher Education Act was followed by further expansion of universities, with smaller HE colleges and other specialist institutions evolving into universities, along with the more recent arrival of private providers. There are now over 150 universities in the UK. Expansion was supposed to offer young people an array of different opportunities suitable to their diverse needs and interests, and enable them to find a suitable HE institution close to home, averting the necessity for expensive long-distance travel. The ending of the old binary divide was also intended to break down old barriers of class and status, making a university education available to everybody who could gain the requisite advanced level qualifications. This was a further step in developing a mass HE system, symbolized powerfully in the target of 50 % of young people participating in some form of HE.

In reality, over the decades since 1992, the various universities have fought to distinguish themselves from each other, which they have attempted in a variety of ways: by developing specific mission statements, by announcing an international or conversely a local focus, by grouping themselves into lobbying alliances (the Russell Group, Million+, University Alliance and so forth) and, most recently, by focusing on marketing themselves as unique 'brands'. Thus the University of the West of England, one of the two universities studied in this book, announces itself as 'The University for the Real World', while the University of Bristol emphasizes its leading position in rankings for research and global success. At the top of the tree, the 'Golden Triangle' of Cambridge, Oxford and London still constitute an elite tier which acquires a huge proportion of available research funding and can attract the best qualified undergraduates who hope to be taught by research stars and renowned professors. Of course, they also hope to benefit from the social prestige of an 'Oxbridge' or 'London University' degree.

Contradictorily, at the same time as jockeying for position in a field which is deeply hierarchical, universities have, under sustained pressure from governments, also devoted their energies to widening participation (WP), seeking to open up their programmes to working-class and minority ethnic young people, and other designated groups who are under-represented in HE, such as people with disabilities, young carers, and people who have been in care (https://www.offa.org.uk/press/frequently-asked-questions/#definitions).

The UK Government sets targets for each institution, based on the current composition of the student body, to recruit an increasing number of disadvantaged young people. Various measures are used to identify students from a disadvantaged or WP background, including postcode, parents' occupations and levels of educational attainment, and type of school the applicant attended. UoB, the elite university in our study, has the highest number of privately educated students after Oxford and Cambridge and finds it difficult to achieve its WP targets, despite an active WP unit energetically developing strategies to diversify recruitment. The

WP programme has included collaborative working with UWE on some initiatives, and both universities run mentoring schemes, summer schools, and access schemes to encourage applications from under-represented and disadvantaged groups, offer financial support and bursaries, and run networks for local teachers. A joint working group of researchers and administrators with this common interest across the two universities has met regularly since 2006/2007, with the *Paired Peers* project as one major outcome (Hoare et al. 2011).

So have things really changed since Brown and Scase carried out their study? Are working-class students still a rarity in elite universities? Are they channelled into more vocational subjects (outside of the traditional, highly regarded vocations of medicine and law), which are more likely to be offered at post-1992 institutions? When they arrive at university, do they still stand out as anomalies? Or conversely, do they integrate themselves into the social life of the more privileged students? Are the universities in the business of promoting social mobility through their WP procedures? Or are they still helping to reproduce the existing class structure, dominated by an aggressively self-promoting elite, which justifies its existence by utilizing the neo-liberal values of 'choice', meritocracy and entitlement, as argued by commentators including the UK government's mobility 'tsar', Alan Milburn, *Guardian* journalists Owen Jones and Aditya Chakraborty, and academics Danny Dorling and Andrew Sayer? We sought to answer these questions amongst others in a largely qualitative research project, which investigated the experiences of a group of students from contrasting class backgrounds who we tracked through three years of undergraduate study at two differing universities.

The Paired Peers Study: Class and the Student Experience

The *Paired Peers* project was a three-year study funded by the Leverhulme Trust. It started in 2010, as the recession really started to bite in Britain, and two years before the upper limit of tuition fees to be paid by students was raised from £3000 a year to £9000 in 2012. The study followed a cohort of students who were embarking on degrees at Bristol's two universities, UoB and UWE. The aim was to observe how their experience of HE and the resources they brought into and acquired within HE were shaped by their social-class backgrounds. By doing this, we hoped to understand more fully the obstacles as well as the opportunities that might be placed in the way of young people from working-class backgrounds in not only accessing but also reaping the benefits of HE, and to contrast their experiences with those of their middle-class peers. This would inform the broader aim of assessing the role of universities in helping to build a fairer and more open society.

Our study was guided by the following key questions:

1. What were the experiences of undergraduate study of a sample of working-class and middle-class students at two differently positioned universities located in one city in England?
2. What kind of capitals did students bring into university with them (economic, social and cultural) and how were they able to develop and mobilize different forms of capital during their university years?
3. What can we learn from this understanding of the student experience about the ways in which university study promotes, or does not promote, social mobility?

Our research was based on a strategy of matching pairs. Students were recruited from a range of those subject disciplines taught at both of the universities in the study. Once we had identified these disciplines and gained their permission to approach students, we sought to recruit four students in each subject from each university, two from working-class and two from middle-class backgrounds. Thus we could compare the fortunes of middle- and working-class students from UoB, with their equivalents at UWE.

To identify potential participants, two researchers visited each department during the universities' induction weeks and addressed the body of first-year students, telling them about the project and inviting them to become participants in the three-year study. All students present at these sessions were asked to complete a short questionnaire collecting demographic details that were based on those used by UCAS to identify students from a WP background: parents' education and occupations, postcode, type of school attended, receipt of maintenance grant or bursaries, as well as their own class identification. They were asked to give contact details if they were prepared to take part in the research. We then categorized all those who volunteered as being either working-class, middle-class or difficult to classify, what we came to refer to as 'the muddle in the middle'. The latter contradictory or in-between class positions of course reflect the fact that class identification is highly complex, 'essentially contested' and volatile (Bradley 2016; Roberts 2011), an issue which will be discussed more fully in Chapter 2.

Using these categorizations, we were able to recruit 90 students for an initial interview, drawn from 11 disciplines: biological sciences, drama, economics and accountancy, engineering, English, geography, history, law, politics, psychology and sociology. We aimed here to cover a range of disciplines, and to include sciences, arts and social sciences, though our choice was restricted by the requirement that both universities needed to offer these subjects. We slightly over-recruited, anticipating that there would inevitably be some dropout over the three years, as was indeed the case. Our target was 80, we recruited 90, and we managed to retain 70 throughout the three years of the project. Each student was interviewed twice in each year of study, and we also collected additional data through focus groups, diaries, records of a typical week in their university life, photographs, and maps which showed the students' individual use of the city. We analysed our data using the qualitative data analysis software program NVivo. We developed a coding manual, with themes and codes identified using previous literature and research. These were refined and extended as a result of fieldwork, and ongoing analysis of our data, so that as the project progressed, we revised and updated the coding manual. All members of the research team were involved in coding and analysing data, and we used the manual to help us clarify our understandings as a team, and to ensure that we applied codes in a similar way.

At the end of each year of the project, we held a social event to which all the participants were invited. Around 30 attended each event. We provided food and drink, organized games, offered prizes, and told them a little bit about the findings of that phase of the research. This gave the participants a chance to get to know some of the other students and to meet the whole of the research team. We believed that this was one of the ways in which we could build a sense of commitment to the research, and that did seem to be the case as the social events were a great success. It also allowed us to get to know the students better in a more informal setting.

Attrition is of course a problem with any longitudinal research study, and we used various strategies to limit dropout. Aside from the social events, students were rewarded each year with a book token. We suggested that the project might be a way to learn something about the process of doing empirical research, and that they could include participation in the project on their CV. As we anticipated, the largest drop out was in the first year. Over the course of the project, five students abandoned their courses, and one suspended study for a year. Of these, three were middle-class, three working-class; three were female and three male, and five were from UWE, which has a higher overall dropout rate than Bristol. In addition, after the initial interviews, 12 could not be contacted again. We presume they were caught up in student life and felt they could not make the time commitment to the study; it is also possible that some of them left university.

After the first year the cohort stabilized, though some students would miss one of the interviews, usually because of being overwhelmed with work or going through some particular personal crisis. However, most of those who remained built up a strong attachment to the project and many told us that they enjoyed the chance to talk through their experiences with a sympathetic outsider. Indeed, the secret of the success of the project, in our view, was the rapport established by our interviewers with the students they were assigned to interview. Not all interviews are successful: we were lucky to recruit skilled and sensitive researchers into our team. They were able to build strong relationships and get the students to talk frankly and freely about their lives.

Bristol's two universities, where the study was based, are both of high standing, but are very different in style and in the students they target. UoB is a traditional research-intensive university and a member of the elite Russell Group of universities. Its Vice-Chancellor at the time of the research, Sir Eric Thomas, was for a time the chair of Universities UK, the employers' association. It is particularly strong on the science side, and has a large medical school and law school, but also covers the full range of traditional arts, humanities and social science subjects. It has high entrance requirements and is an extremely popular student choice, with many applicants per place in some of its subjects. It has a large number of buildings spread across central areas of the city, most of them in Clifton and Cotham, though there are outliers such as the Veterinary School at Long Ashton. Some of these buildings are rather old, not to say archaic. Some, such as the Law School in the striking Wills Memorial Building with its tower that dominates the central city skyline, are rather magnificent. The UoB students tended to appreciate the traditional aura of such buildings.

In contrast, UWE is a modern university and a member of the University Alliance mission group, which is currently chaired by UWE's Vice-Chancellor, Steve West. While UoB has its eyes on the international research community, UWE has taken pride in its role within the city and region, building up strong links with local businesses. It has more vocational subjects than Bristol, including a large number of healthcare-related degrees, along with creative arts based on a separate campus.

It has no medical school, but a very large Faculty of Business and Law, which attracts numbers of home and international students. It currently has three sites, but the main campus is located on the fringe of Bristol and is surrounded by a student village, and is said to be one of the largest in Europe. The buildings on the main site are modern and more conventionally suited for teaching than those of UoB. UWE participants in the project appeared to like the on-site facilities of bars, cafes and shops, which, because of the isolation of the site, are more extensive than those of UoB. They liked the idea of having accommodation close to the university and told us that they felt a strong sense of welcome when they first visited to attend open days.

As one might suspect from these descriptions, the class composition of the two universities is very different, though in 2010/2011, when the participants in the *Paired Peers* project commenced undergraduate study, UWE still had fewer working-class students compared to the UK average (Table 1.1).

In some of the UoB departments included in our study there were only a limited number of students we could categorize as working-class. As we will see in subsequent chapters, some working-class students found it hard to adapt within this environment and, over the years, some talented students left and transferred to other less notably 'posh' universities. By contrast, UWE's student body is more mixed and diverse and most students are able to find companions with whom they feel at ease. Chapters 4 and 5 highlight this issue of social 'fit' and its impact on the student participants.

Class and Education: The Sociological Context

Our study is located within the growing body of research publications which deal with class and education. Although class fell out of favour in

Table 1.1 Student intake by social class in 2010/2011 at UoB, UWE, and UK national average

	UoB (per cent)	UWE (per cent)	UK average (per cent)
Middle-class (NS-SEC 1–3)	86	71	69
Working-class (NS-SEC 4–7)	14	29	31

Source: https://www.hesa.ac.uk/pis/urg

the 1980s and 1990s as a central topic for sociology, the last 20 years have seen a major revival of interest both in class theory and in empirical research on class differences. Although this interest has been heightened by the rapid increases of wealth and income for the richest strata in society under the Conservative-Liberal Democrat Coalition government of 2010–2015, much of the impetus for what has been called the New Sociology of Class (Bradley 2016) came from within university education departments, where scholars such as Stephen Ball and Diane Reay were exploring the continued salience of class in relation to educational experience and attainment at various levels. This fed into theoretical work being developed by sociologists such as Mike Savage and Beverley Skeggs. All were utilizing the ideas of French sociologist Pierre Bourdieu in this re-exploration of class division and class reproduction. In particular, this work explored the role of various forms of capital—economic, social, cultural and symbolic—in reproducing the hierarchies of class and attendant privileges or disadvantages, as set out in Bourdieu's text *Distinction* (1984). As detailed in Chapter 2, Bourdieu's concepts of *habitus, capital* and *field* became central to the thinking of these scholars.

In terms of our study, three bodies of work concerned with the effects of widening participation in HE have informed our thinking: research on differentiation and stratification of HE; studies of undergraduate experience, focusing especially on class differences; and work on graduate labour markets. The extensive literature in these areas is not fully reviewed here. Rather, we draw attention to key themes that are particularly relevant to our study.

The mass expansion of HE is defined by Shavit et al. (2007) as one of the most important social transformations of the second half of the twentieth century. It holds out the promise of opening up access to working-class and other disadvantaged groups, and is crucially important for what we have called 'the degree generation', who live at a time when knowledge is seen as the key to competing for economic prosperity in a globalized world. But mass expansion does not mean that the whole system serves equally a 'mass' population of students (where, following Trow (1973) up to 50 % of a relevant age group participate). HE systems in the twenty-first century involve elite and mass forms of HE at the same time, with different parts of the system functioning in different ways, and serving different purposes (Bathmaker and Thomas 2009; Moodie 2009).

A key question for research into widening access and social stratification, then, is whether expansion reduces or conversely maintains and produces new forms of inequality, even while allowing working-class and other disadvantaged groups access to HE (Mayhew et al. 2004; Osborne et al. 2007; Shavit et al. 2007; Teichler 2007, 2008; Vignoles and Crawford 2010). For while expansion has indeed opened up the HE field, it has been accompanied by hierarchical differentiation of institutions: the status and value of different forms of HE are not equal in relation to one another. Who goes where and who does what are therefore important considerations (Reay et al. 2005), with implications for future progression. Croxford and Raffe (2015, p. 1626) sum up what is at stake here:

> As HE expands, the mere fact of going to university no longer ensures access to future elites; the type of institution attended also matters.

Studies of student experience have pursued these questions further, focusing on how structures shape the actions and behaviours of students, both in their decisions to progress to HE and their experience of participating in it. While there is an increasing amount of work offering statistical analyses of patterns of access, participation and progression (e.g. Boliver 2011, 2013; Chowdry et al. 2010; OFFA 2014; UCAS 2014), only a small number of studies have focused in-depth on student experience and social class in the context of an expanded system. In England, work by a team from London Metropolitan University at the beginning of the 2000s (Archer et al. 2003) looked in detail at patterns of participation under expansion, and discussed the potential reasons for the under-representation of working-class groups in HE. A subsequent study by Reay et al. (2005) explored HE choice and decision-making and highlighted how working-class students face differing degrees of choice that are significantly shaped by their social class.

More recently, a study by Crozier, Reay and Clayton has investigated the experiences of working-class undergraduates studying a range of subjects in four different HE institutions in England, ranging from an elite university to a college of further education (Reay et al. 2009, 2010; Crozier and Reay 2011), once again, drawing attention to the challenges and barriers that working-class students face. In Canada, Lehmann (2009, 2013) has similarly considered the experience of working-class students while at university, while Burke (2015), in research comparable to ours, has contrasted the experience and trajectories of working-class and middle-class students in Northern

Ireland. All these studies indicate how HE continues to be fraught with uncertainty for the working-classes, even when they are deemed to be successful university students.

As the evolving focus of the above studies demonstrates, while access to HE was a key concern as the system expanded, developing into an interest in the classed nature of student experience once in HE, recent attention has turned to progression beyond HE, the growing competition for graduate level jobs, and the stark inequalities in access to the professions. Despite regularly cited evidence of the returns to individuals of participation in HE (BIS 2010; Walker and Zhu 2013), a large national study by Purcell and colleagues, which tracked students who commenced undergraduate study in England in 2006 through to their destinations in 2011/2012, found both increased levels of graduate unemployment, and also strong evidence that graduates are taking non-graduate jobs, in which they do not consider their graduate skills and knowledge to be useful (Purcell et al. 2013).

The effect of increasing competition for jobs, according to work by Brown and colleagues since the early 2000s, is that middle-class families in particular adopt increasingly desperate measures to 'stay ahead' of the competition for future employment (Brown et al. 2003; Brown and Hesketh 2004; Brown et al. 2011; Brown and Tannock 2009). A degree is no longer enough, and students are urged to mobilize different forms of 'capital' during their undergraduate study, through participation in extra-curricular activities (ECA), work experience and internships, in order to enhance their future social and economic positioning. A range of work exploring engagement in ECA indicates that new hurdles are created through unequal access or capacity to take up such opportunities (Allen et al. 2013; Bathmaker et al. 2013; Jonsson et al. 2009; Lehmann 2012; Swartz 2008). Unpaid internships in particular have been in the public eye, with the chair of the UK's social mobility commission emphasizing that 'they further disadvantage those from less affluent backgrounds who cannot afford to work for free for any length of time.' (Milburn 2012, p. 5).

Meanwhile, inequalities in gaining access to the professions, particularly elite levels of professions such as law and financial services, have been the subject of a number of recent studies (Ashley and Empson 2013; Browne 2010; Cook et al. 2012; Friedman et al. 2015; Macmillan and Vignoles 2013; Macmillan et al. 2015; Wakeling and Savage 2015), and a particular focus of attention for the UK's Social Mobility and Child

Poverty Commission (Milburn 2009, 2012; SMCP 2014; McKnight 2015). All of these expose clear and continuing patterns of privilege. In 2009 Milburn stated:

> Many of the UK's professions have become more socially exclusive and as a consequence, bright children from average-income families, not just those from more disadvantaged backgrounds, are missing out on a professional career. (2009, p. 12)

Three years later, little appeared to have changed. In a follow-up report, Milburn (2012, p. 3) commented, 'Across the professions as a whole, the glass ceiling has been scratched but not broken.' And in 2015, a further report stated that access to elite professional firms remained unequal and 'professional employees generally have privileged backgrounds in comparison to the UK population' (Ashley et al. 2015, p. 9).

Our study aims to further contribute to understandings of how class permeates the structures and experience of HE. We focus on how social class plays out in the lives of students in two differently positioned universities in the English HE system, and the ways in which class shapes their preparation for transition to future lives and employment. Our focus engages with questions of how HE may promote or contribute to social mobility, placing us on challenging terrain. Previous research alerts us to how questions of HE and social mobility can quickly become conflated with a project of how to become middle-class (Lehmann 2009; Loveday 2015; Reay 2012). Loveday comments:

> The university is often understood as 'saving' the working-class subject 'from themselves and their lives' and this is achieved by transforming them into more middle-class versions of their selves through the provision of 'forms of capital'. (2015, p. 583)

Our intention is not to work out how working-class students can 'escape' their working-class backgrounds. We are, however, interested in how and whether HE constitutes part of a process of mobility. This relates not just to working-class students. As Roberts (2010) has observed, HE has become a means of strengthening the distinction between an upper middle-class and the rest of the middle-classes. Moreover, in the 2010s, austerity measures, involving extensive cuts to public services as well as wider job insecurities, have affected the middle-classes as well as the working-classes, whose concerns about downward mobility may result in 'opportunity hoarding' (McKnight 2015; Reeves and Howard 2013; Waller 2011; Waller et al. 2014). In this context HE might be understood as part of a project concerned with how to *stay* middle-class and avoid downward mobility as much as a route to *becoming* middle-class.

THE STRUCTURE OF THE BOOK

The chapters that follow look at the findings of our study of HE and social class and explore the experiences of the student participants. Chapter 2 discusses the complexities involved in researching and classifying class and class identifications and explains how social class was operationalized in the *Paired Peers* project. Chapter 3 further sets the context of the study by exploring the embedding of the universities and their students in the city of Bristol and examining the characteristics of the two student bodies. We show how belonging to one or other of the two universities shapes young people's identities and experiences of the city. Chapters 4–7 draw extensively on the interview material to explore the experiences of participants over three years of study, examining the impact of class and also gender on their experiences and their progress. Chapter 4 looks at the routes the students took to get into university and their initial experiences of settling in to student life; Chapter 5 explores how the experiences of university were differentiated for students from different class backgrounds and how that affected their sense of belonging and their involvement in the extra-curricular activities on offer; while Chapter 6 considers their career ambitions and looks at their first steps on the road into jobs in the context of the acute competition for well-paid graduate jobs. We call these chapters 'Getting In', 'Getting On' and 'Getting Out', echoing the similar usage in Phil Brown's book on education and the working-class *Schooling Ordinary Kids* (Brown 1987). Chapter 7 looks at how students from Black, Asian and Minority Ethnic (BAME) backgrounds experienced social relationships within the two universities and reflects on the meaning of ethnicity in these young people's lives, highlighting the normalcy of whiteness. Chapter 8 concludes the study, reflecting on the potentially transformative experience of HE and the possibilities for social mobility embedded within it, ending with implications for social policies on widening participation and the provision of tertiary education. Although this book forms a continuous narrative, we hope that readers will feel free to dip into particular chapters that are of special interest to them, and thus we have attempted to make each chapter readable as a stand-alone discussion.

CONCLUDING COMMENTS

> I think there's a lot attached to the sort of higher education you've been through, there's a difference in whether you've been to polytechnic and got a degree there, whether you've been to university or whether you've been to Oxbridge. (Brown and Scase 1994, p. 79)

> If you had an Oxbridge degree it means you're quality… it's a status symbol in itself, it means, I suppose you're good because otherwise they wouldn't accept you. (ibid., p. 75)

This was how two of the students interviewed in the Brown and Scase study summed up the hierarchy within HE in the early 1990s. One of the reasons for the ending of the binary divide in 1992 was to challenge the status gap between the polytechnics and universities. As Brown and Scase make clear, this distinction of prestige and its impact on employment chances was clearly correlated to the class backgrounds of the various student bodies: Oxbridge for the elite, redbrick and plate-glass universities for the middle-classes, and polytechnics with their vocational slant for people from working-class families. One of the objectives of this book is to explore whether this educational hierarchy still persists. The methodology of the *Paired Peers* study, which has been outlined in this chapter, enables us to explore the experiences and progress of working-class and middle-class students in two universities differently situated in the current status hierarchy. The chapters explore the participants' fortunes: do students of different classes feel at home in both types of university? Does their progress and achievement vary by class? And does it still make a difference whether you go to UoB or UWE?

Jones (2014) is one of many writers who have argued that the more prestigious universities, notably Oxford and Cambridge, but also some leading universities in the Russell Group such as Bristol and Durham, are still the training and recruiting grounds for 'the establishment': members of the dominant classes who control politics, the media, and occupy top posts in the professions and the major corporations—what Mills (1956) termed 'the power elite'. The persistence of hierarchical attitudes amongst the 'Oxbridge elite' is reflected in recent pronouncements from some of its alumni. Julian Fellowes, the writer of the popular TV series *Downton Abbey*, declared that those without university degrees could not understand the plays of Shakespeare, while Labour MP and historian Tristram Hunt told Cambridge University students that as members of the top 1 %, it is they who should be running the Labour Party, rather than people without degrees or from less prestigious universities.

In subsequent chapters, we use interview data from our study to explore these issues, demonstrating how class background has shaped the experience of being a student for the young women and men who participated in our research. Before this, however, we explain in the next chapter in more detail how class was defined in our research and how we selected our participants. We also explain how class theory, and the work of Pierre Bourdieu, have informed our account of how these young people lived their lives as undergraduates at Bristol's two universities and the ways in which we interpret their actions, ideas and aspirations for the future.

CHAPTER 2

Researching Class and Higher Education

Class, it seems, is everywhere. It spans the length of billboards and broadcasts itself in the media, up close, right in the face of things. It runs through the city and down its segregated highways. It manifests unabashedly on Wall Street and heaps on the corner of Main Street. It has colour. It is what you eat. It resounds through language and its jurisdiction is knowledge. It shapes reputation. It opens and closes doors. It is a roving eye, never dormant. It is with us until the end—in sickness and in health—lengthening or shortening that span. And though seemingly omnipresent it remains strongly absent from the collective conscious. (Stich 2012, p. 105)

INTRODUCTION

The *Paired Peers* project followed undergraduate students at Bristol's two universities for three years from 2010 to 2013, as outlined in Chapter 1. A UK government report published at that time stated:

Children from the most disadvantaged areas are only a third as likely to enter higher education as children from the most advantaged areas, and are less likely to attend the most selective higher education institutions. (Cabinet Office 2011, p. 19)

Yet despite the establishment of a Social Mobility and Child Poverty Commission in 2010 with a clear remit to focus on class inequalities, social class is not considered to be a legally protected characteristic under the UK's

© The Editor(s) (if applicable) and The Author(s) 2016   21
A.M. Bathmaker et al., *Higher Education, Social Class and Social Mobility*, DOI 10.1057/978-1-137-53481-1_2

2010 Equality Act, unlike gender, race and sexuality. It is not, therefore, illegal to discriminate against people based on their social class background. Jones (2011) provides a thought-provoking analysis of the effects of this in his book *Chavs: the demonization of the working class*. He argues that we have become accepting of class mockery and insult, even though the effects of poverty and material disadvantage are real and pervasive.

In this chapter, we discuss the way in which we operationalized a definition of class in order to carry out our objective of comparing the experiences of working-class and middle-class students at the two universities in the study. This is no easy task. How social class is conceptualized and defined is the subject of intense debates at the present time, and we explain how these debates have informed the understanding of social class in our study. In the second part of the chapter, we go on to discuss how we used the work of Bourdieu in our analysis of class and students' experience of HE.

DEFINING AND REDEFINING SOCIAL CLASS

In January 2011, the Great British Class Survey, launched by the BBC, received 161,400 responses. The survey not only demonstrated the strength of public interest in social class in the twenty-first century, it was also indicative of current debates about the construction of social class, and the role of social and cultural processes in generating class divisions. The web-based survey, developed by sociologists Mike Savage, Fiona Devine and colleagues, aimed to develop a new model of social class (Savage et al. 2013, 2015), combining measures of economic, cultural and social capital in order to map contemporary class divisions. Although subsequent critiques (e.g. Dorling 2014b; Mills 2014; Skeggs 2015) suggest flaws in the model proposed by Savage and colleagues, they also highlight the continuing salience of class to our understanding of inequalities and mobility, particularly at a time of increasing economic and social inequalities throughout the world, and the spread of austerity policies in the UK and elsewhere across the globe.

This work formed part of what has been called a cultural turn in social class research, to which the work of Bourdieu has made a key contribution. Bourdieu (1987) argues that individuals are positioned in social space in relation to others, based on the amount and type of symbolically recognized capital to which they have access. His work identifies three key forms of capital: economic, cultural and social (Bourdieu 1997). Economic capital involves financial resources and may be institutionalized, in the form of property rights for example. Social capital consists of a person's networks or connections, which can be institutionalized as a 'title of nobility'. Cultural capital occurs in three forms: institutionalized, as educational qualifications for example; objectified, in the material possession of cultural goods such as books, pictures and instruments; and embodied, in the form of habitus and long-lasting dispositions of the mind and body. While the varieties of cultural capital are numerous, certain forms are considered more legitimate or valuable than others in a given social field. Moreover, some forms of cultural capital, such as academic capabilities, may be unrecognized as capital, and instead perceived to be legitimate competence, and functioning as what Bourdieu refers to as 'symbolic capital' (1997, p. 49). Cultural and social capitals can never be entirely reduced to economic capital, but Bourdieu writes that their power comes from the fact that they are intrinsically tied to economic capital, though this connection is disguised. Class then is not about economic capital in a straightforward way, but involves cultural and social capitals that position individuals in social space advantageously or disadvantageously in relation to others.

Whilst this cultural turn in class analysis was revolutionary, a major problem facing researchers attempting to utilize Bourdieusian theory to measure social class is that the forms of capital—in particular cultural and social—are difficult to quantify and operationalize (Vryonides 2007). So despite strong evidence that class is more than about the economic, official definitions in Britain today still rely on an occupational scheme, the National Statistics Socio-Economic Classification (NS-SEC), though recent research such as that of Savage and colleagues, and also Atkinson and Rosenlund (2014) looks for new ways in which Bourdieu's theorizing can be translated into a method for classifying society. Based on their analysis of the Great British Class Survey, which included detailed questions on social, cultural and economic capital, Savage and colleagues propose that it is possible to divide contemporary British society into seven major classes. They write:

> We demonstrate the existence of an 'elite', whose wealth separates them from an established middle class, as well as a class of technical experts and a class of 'new affluent' workers. We also show that at the lower levels of the class structure, alongside an ageing traditional working class, there is a 'precariat' characterised by very low levels of capital, and a group of emergent service workers. We think that this new seven class model recognises both social polarization in British society and class fragmentation in its middle layers. (Savage et al. 2013, p. 1)

Their work has opened up extensive debate, including much criticism for the way in which it removes the economic and relational element of class and seems to define social classes based on the product and outcomes of class inequality (e.g. Bradley 2014). For their part, Savage and colleagues acknowledge that their class scheme is inductive rather than deductive (that is, it derives from the way they located clusters of individuals in their survey in 'social space' and not from any prior theory of how class relations operate) and thus it cannot be simply applied as a new national framework for classifying people. They argue that it is not meant to replace the occupationally-based NS-SEC, rather that the scheme sheds light on the ways in which class works through the cultural and social field as well as the economic (Savage et al. 2013).

The rest of this chapter discusses how we engaged with social class as a cultural as well as an economic phenomenon in the *Paired Peers* project, in order to understand the experience of students in HE. We start with how we identified the social class of participants in the study, using a number of indicators commonly used in the context of UK HE. We then go on to discuss how we worked with Bourdieu's concepts of field, capital and habitus, and developments of his ideas, in order to analyse our longitudinal data on students' experience of moving into and through the field of HE.

ASSIGNING CLASS POSITIONS TO PARTICIPANTS IN THE *PAIRED PEERS* PROJECT

Our aim in the fieldwork was to identify an equal number of UK students from working-class and middle-class backgrounds at the two universities in Bristol (UWE and UoB), who would participate in the study for the following three years. Our sample was drawn from 11 subjects that were taught at both universities (biological sciences, drama, economics and accountancy, engineering, English, geography, history, law, politics, psychology and sociology). Focusing on these subjects presented us with something of a challenge in identifying enough participants from a working-class background. Some previous research suggests that the fields of study chosen by students can be socially stratified. Those from a family background with a high level of education may tend to study subjects that traditionally award high status to graduates and are financially rewarding, such as law and medicine, or they study general academic subjects in the arts, social sciences or humanities, that have no clearly defined link to occupations, but act as a screening mechanism, whereby employers can select people for the broad attributes, capacities and potential that they require, rather than specific knowledge and skills (Moodie et al. 2015). In contrast, those from lower socio-economic backgrounds may pursue fields of study that appear to offer a safe pathway to employment, such as business and administration, and health and social care (Bohonnek et al. 2010; Van de Werfhorst et al. 2003). Working-class students are therefore not necessarily evenly represented across the HE field, and the participants in the *Paired Peers* project were from particular parts of this field.

In order to identify participants, we administered a questionnaire to all first-year students at the start of their undergraduate course, which gathered background and demographic information that we used to classify students by social class, as well as asking for volunteers to participate over the next three years. 2124 questionnaires were completed, of which 1773 were UK students. 42 % of the UK respondents volunteered to participate further. The key variables that we used to classify students were the occupations of parents; participation in HE by parents; receipt of maintenance grant or bursary; and self-assigned social class.

We used NS-SEC to classify parents' occupations by class. NS-SEC is the system currently used by the UK's Office for National Statistics. Based on a class schema, which was developed in the 1970s by a team from Nuffield College Oxford, led by John Goldthorpe (Goldthorpe et al. 1980), it places people into classes according to their occupation and also their employment status. For example, while a 'self-employed plumber' and a 'foreman plumber' both share the same occupational *function*, their employment *status* differs. The system was first used in the 2001 census (Crompton 2008) and subsequently revised in 2010. The current NS-SEC is made up of eight categories, ranging from higher managerial, administrative and professional occupations including employers in large organizations (class 1) through to long-term unemployed and never worked (class 8). In the project, respondents with parents from NS-SEC classes 1–3 were classified as middle-class, while those from classes 4–8 were classified as working-class.

Based on this classification, 89 % of respondents overall were categorized as middle-class, (95 % of responses from UoB and 80 % of responses from UWE; see Table 2.1).

In addition to using NS-SEC to classify parents' occupations as a key indicator of our participants' class position, we also asked for information about parents' participation in HE. This not only provided a further basis for assigning students to a social class position, but also gave us

Table 2.1 NS-SEC classification of questionnaire respondents based on both parents' occupations

	UoB (%)	UWE (%)	Total (%)
Middle-class (NS-SEC 1–3)	95	80	88
Working-class (NS-SEC 4–8)	5	20	12
Total number of responses	1043	834	1877

some knowledge of the cultural resources that were available in students' families. We further asked students whether they received financial support either from the government in the form of a maintenance grant, or a bursary from their university. However, there are some problems with this as an indicator of class, since it is based on income level (thus the child of an unemployed, divorced middle-class woman might qualify). We gained additional indications about students' backgrounds by asking for information on home post-code, which gave us information about the neighbourhoods the students had come from; the type of school (or college) attended (state or private); and finally the students' own definition of their social class. Thus we sought to develop a multi-factoral approach to defining class (Bradley and Hebson 2000). Parents' occupations and educational level were the main indicators we used, and we turned to the other indicators where we were still doubtful.

For the purposes of identifying participants for the remainder of the study, we sorted questionnaires from those who had volunteered to participate into three categories: middle-class, working-class and contradictory or unclear. The middle-class group included those in NS-SEC classes 1–3, with at least one parent who had completed HE. The majority of them were not in receipt of a maintenance grant or bursary. The working-class group included those in NS-SEC classes 4–8, with no parent who had participated in HE, and in some cases, though not all, stating that they were in receipt of a maintenance grant or bursary. A third group included those responses that we could not classify in a straightforward way, either because we were not confident about classifying the response given regarding parental occupations, or because there were contradictions across the indicators we used. Assigning students to a category of middle-class or working-class was completed collectively, with the research team cross-checking decisions made about allocations. This process enabled us to recruit 90 students at the start of the project, 46 from UWE and 44

Table 2.2 Project participants from UoB and UWE by social class and gender

	UWE working-class	UWE middle-class	UoB working-class	UoB middle-class
Female	12	11	15	11
Male	12	11	6	12
Total	24	22	21	23

Table 2.3 Number of parents reported to have attended university

Parents' experience of HE	UWE working-class	UWE middle-class	UoB working-class	UoB middle-class
none	24	1	19	0
One parent only	0	9	1	9
Both parents	0	12	1	14
Total	24	22	21	23

from UoB, all of whom, based on their questionnaire responses, could be securely assigned to a category of middle-class or working-class, as shown in Table 2.2.

Table 2.3 summarizes details of their parents' experience of HE, showing experience of HE for parents that a student was living with prior to starting university. The table shows that our sample was fairly evenly matched across the two institutions in terms of social class and parental participation in HE.

In both institutions, the vast majority our working-class sample came from families with no HE tradition whilst the middle-class sample, with the exception of one student, had at least one graduate parent (see Appendix 1 for information on the family background of each participant in the project). This indicates a stark contrast in the forms of institutionalized cultural capital between the different classes in our sample (which is of course a product of our sampling method which was designed to select on the basis of the different forms of capital highlighted above).

In the rest of the book, we identify students as either middle-class or working-class based on this initial classification. This allows us to consider classed differences in moving into and through the field of HE—getting in, getting on and getting out of university. However, we are aware that our binary classification masks fractions within classes that have been identified in most forms of class theory, including that of Bourdieu, which further differentiate students' positions and their orientations to HE.

Classic Weberian analysis identifies fractions in the working-class on the basis of their skill (skilled, semi-skilled and unskilled) (Bradley 2016). Savage and colleagues in earlier work (Fielding et al. 1995) distinguished between a managerial, predominantly private sector, fraction of the middle-class with high levels of economic capital, and a professional, often public sector, fraction characterized by high levels of cultural capital. Their account was influenced by the work of Bourdieu (1984), for whom classes are divided internally according to the relative preponderance of economic or cultural capitals possessed by incumbents. Weininger (2002) summarizes Bourdieu's understanding of class fractions as follows. Occupational categories within the dominant class are differentiated from one another such that professors and "artistic producers"—the occupations whose incumbents hold the greatest cultural capital and the least economic capital—are opposed to industrialists and commercial employers—the occupations whose incumbents hold a preponderance of economic capital but relatively little cultural capital. Located in between these two polar extremes are the professions, whose incumbents have roughly equal amounts of economic and social capital. In a similar manner, the petty bourgeoisie is differentiated between small business owners, endowed primarily with economic capital, and primary school teachers, endowed primarily with cultural capital. Located in an intermediate position between them are categories such as technicians, office workers, and secretaries.

In the *Paired Peers* study, differences amongst students based on this more specific account of social class background became increasingly apparent in the students' narratives. In Chapters 4–7, we draw out these more subtle differences, showing how these variations in the social class positioning of students' families can be traced through into how students oriented themselves to HE, and the differences in how they were able to take advantage of the opportunities that HE can offer.

In addition, we were alert to how intersections of gender and class in particular, and also intersections of race, gender and class, shaped the experience of students. We have written about intersections of gender and class elsewhere (Bradley 2012, 2016; Ingram 2009, 2011). The ways in which these intersections work become evident in Chapters 4–6, which explore students' experience in detail. 'Race' was a less overtly visible theme in our data, but in order not to lose sight of the ways in which 'race' and, in particular, 'whiteness' have a significant, though often unspoken, place in students' movement through the field of HE, Chapter 7 focuses specifically on intersections of class and race.

A key strength of our project was being able to follow students over three years of undergraduate study. At the same time, we are aware that volunteering to participate in a longitudinal study requires enthusiasm and willingness to engage with a research project, and the sample that we followed for three years consisted of students who were prepared to spend time reflecting on their undergraduate experience as they progressed through HE. In the final section of this chapter, we discuss briefly working with Bourdieu in the project.

WORKING WITH BOURDIEU IN THE *PAIRED PEERS* PROJECT

Field, Capital and Habitus

Bourdieu's work uses the notion of *field*, along with the concepts of *capital* and *habitus*, to understand social practice, and specifically to uncover the workings of power and inequality in particular social spaces (see Bathmaker 2015). For Bourdieu, a field is a particular social space that involves a network or configuration of relations between positions (Bourdieu 1985, 1998). What positions agents or institutions within a field is the possession of capital and power that is relevant to the purposes of a particular field.

Cultural capital is especially important in the field of education. Bourdieu explains that he initially developed the concept in his work on differences in academic achievement:

> The notion of cultural capital initially presented itself to me, in the course of research, as a theoretical hypothesis which made it possible to explain the unequal scholastic achievement of children originating from the different social classes by relating academic success, i.e., the specific profits which children from the different classes and class fractions can obtain in the academic market, to the distribution of cultural capital between the classes and class fractions. This starting point implies a break with the presuppositions inherent both in the common sense view, which sees academic success or failure as an effect of natural aptitudes, and in human capital theories. (Bourdieu 1997, p. 47)

An important characteristic of cultural capital for Bourdieu is heredita-bility. He argues that while cultural capital makes a substantial contribution to the inter-generational reproduction of class positions, 'the social conditions of its transmission and acquisition are more disguised than those of economic capital' (Bourdieu 1997, p. 49). More recently, Lareau's (2011) research suggests that efforts to ensure the transmission of cultural capital are growing more visible and overt. In her research into the practices of middle-class families in the USA, she talks of the 'concerted cultivation' of capital, whereby families continually work on their children to create an individual with the right capitals to succeed in life. We go on to discuss later in this book, how some middle-class students, when they move into HE, build on the concerted cultivation of capitals they have experienced in the family in their efforts to stay ahead. We refer to this as '*hypermobilization*' of capitals. It involves not just cultural capital, but economic and social capital as well, which work together to enable success in HE, and help sustain class position and privilege.

To understand practice in a particular field, Bourdieu also uses the concept of habitus, which he defines as:

> A system of dispositions, that is of permanent manners of being, seeing, acting, thinking or a system of long lasting (rather than permanent) schemes or schemata or structures of perception, conception and action. (Bourdieu 2002, p. 27)

Habitus is 'the learned set of preferences or dispositions by which a person orients to the social world' (Edgerton and Roberts 2014, p. 195). It is about tastes, practices and dispositions. It is about language and how we carry ourselves. Bourdieu (1990, p. 70) writes of habitus that it involves: '*ways of standing, speaking, walking and thereby feeling and thinking*'. Habitus is individual but it is also collective (Bourdieu 1990), involving similarities with others based on experiences that are common to members of the same class. Class therefore manifests itself through the habitus and shapes a person's being in a particular social space, hence a 'class-specific habitus' (Lareau and Weininger 2003, p. 379). Nash (2002) talks of an educated habitus, which involves characteristics such as a positive orientation to schooling, high aspirations, a positive academic self-concept, and a desire to identify and be identified as educated. This educated habitus can also be class-specific, based on a classed view of education and its value, and could be considered the manifestation of an amalagam of institutionalized, objectified and embodied cultural capital.

Moving into a new social field, such as HE, will be easier for those where there is 'habitus-field congruence' (Ingram 2009), that is the dispositions of habitus align well with a particular field, and an individual feels like a 'fish in water' (Bourdieu and Wacquant 1992). The possibility of changing or adapting the habitus particularly when moving into a new field is therefore a key question. Bourdieu highlights the difficulties in changing the habitus. While he argues that a person's habitus can be altered and adapted by new experiences in different social fields, he emphasizes how this can be problematic if the new field is not aligned to the old and can cause a habitus 'divided against itself' wrought with internal conflict and pain (Bourdieu 1999, p. 51). The effects of field-habitus incongruence—of being a fish out of water—are well-documented, but more recently there is also discussion of how rapidly changing social conditions, and much greater social diversity, are leading to evidence of a more flexible, reflexive habitus (Sweetman 2003), and Sweetman argues that an important issue to consider now is how individuals may vary in the capacity to adapt and adjust the habitus.

Habitus, Affect and the Psychosocial Nature of Class

While habitus has helped us to make sense of how class is ingrained in students' dispositions and orientations to HE, Bourdieu's work engages less with the affective dimensions of class, which is a crucial dimension of the student narratives in our project. To help our thinking here, we have turned to the work of Reay (2002, 2004, 2015), Ingram (2011) and Stich (2012) amongst others, who consider the emotional and psychosocial dimensions of class.

Reay (2015) argues that the concept of habitus can be extended to include affective dispositions, so that habitus then becomes a tool for understanding 'the affective dimensions of both privilege and disadvantage' (Reay 2015, p. 21). Including affective dimensions, she argues, enables an understanding of 'how a psychic economy of social class—feelings of ambivalence, inferiority and superiority, visceral aversions, recognition and abjection—is internalized and played out in practices.' (2015, p. 21).

Drawing on Bourdieu's insight that the habitus of the dominant can operate as a means of trying to justify and defend or deny class privilege, Reay emphasizes how conflicts in the habitus can create anxieties for those in both privileged and marginalized positions, particularly where different aspects of multiple habitus clash with each other (such as the home habitus versus the educational habitus). Ingram (2011) talks of this as a habitus tug, where the 'cleft habitus' is in competition within itself as the individual is pulled in multiple directions, resulting in conflict and struggle. However, subsequent work suggests that this sense of conflict can, for some, be reconciled and channelled in positive ways (Abrahams and Ingram 2013; Ingram and Abrahams 2016).

To understand how unequal structures of the HE field create affects, we draw on Stich's work on 'reputational affect' (2012, p. 30). Reputational affect involves the ways in which the popular views, status and positioning of different HE institutions work their way into discourses of students, and help shape their dispositions and practices. The notion of reputational affect therefore draws attention to the emotional and psychosocial aspects of attending an institution in a particular part of the HE field.

Concluding Comments

The *Paired Peers* project seeks to engage with the complexities of class, and the ways in which it shapes the experience of students in HE in England. In order to research their experience we assigned participants to a social class position of middle-class or working-class at the beginning of the project. However, as we learned more about individual participants over the course of three years, we saw how nuances in social class positions shaped their individual lives. While our understandings became more complex, we are confident that our analysis, which draws out the differences in students' experience based on their working-class or middle-class background, has a robust basis in the evidence in our data.

Our analysis in subsequent chapters is informed by Bourdieu's work and his concepts of field, capital and habitus. The development of Bourdieu's ideas by researchers including Reay on habitus and affect (2002, 2004, 2015), Stich on reputational affect (2012), and Lareau (2003, 2011) on the concerted cultivation of capitals by middle-class families, have helped to extend our thinking. Their work has enabled us to identify the contradictions sensed by middle-class as well as working-class students as they progress through the HE field, negotiate the construction of their identities as undergraduate students and prepare themselves for future adulthood.

CHAPTER 3

Two Universities, One City

Introduction

In this chapter, we explore the context in which the *Paired Peers* study took place. We give an account of the two universities in the study within their geographical location, pointing to their different missions and reputational positioning in the field of HE. The contrasting nature of these universities was an important element in our research design as they have different entrance requirements, inducements to study and different learning environments, and their student bodies vary demographically. In other words, each has a very different institutional habitus (Reay 1998), which in turn affects the nature of the student experience, our central topic. This chapter, then, outlines the nature of the two institutions, the characteristics of the students who attend them, and considers how reputational positioning and institutional habitus permeate the ways in which students view each of the universities and understand their position within them.

The *Paired Peers* study was carried out in Bristol, a city in the South West of England. Like many UK cities, Bristol has two universities, the University of Bristol (UoB), a traditional redbrick university (one of those founded in the nineteenth or early twentieth centuries in major British cities), and a newer university, the University of the West of England, Bristol (UWE), which is a former polytechnic. As indicated in Chapter 1, these two universities in Bristol typify many of the widely recognized differences that have continued beyond the 1992 Further and Higher Education Act. UoB is an

© The Editor(s) (if applicable) and The Author(s) 2016

A.M. Bathmaker et al., *Higher Education, Social Class and Social Mobility*, DOI 10.1057/978-1-137-53481-1_3

elite research-intensive university, while UWE Bristol is a modern university, with a focus on teaching as well as research, and having a much larger student population. In 2013/2014, the latest figures available at the time of writing, UWE had 21,000 undergraduate students, compared with 15,000 at the University of Bristol. When the *Paired Peers* cohort arrived in autumn 2010, the difference was greater still: 24,000 students at UWE and 14,000 at UoB.

These two universities also represent a particular example of the institutional stratification of HE in the UK discussed briefly in Chapter 1 that is, the ways in which institutions are hierarchically classified on the basis of features such as their selectivity, emphasis on research and academic prestige (Clark 1978; Moodie 2009; Teichler 1988, 2008). In this chapter, we discuss this stratification in general, and then look in more detail at the two universities, how each institution is positioned in a stratified field of HE, who attends each university, including differences in social class and geographical location, both of which were central to the initial research design and subsequent analysis in the *Paired Peers* project. This stratification goes beyond the mere classifying of universities into different categories, whether based on age of foundation or otherwise, but also, and more significantly, involves embedded perceptions of status and merit, of which their staff, most of the students and indeed the HE community at large are all too well aware.

THE EVOLVING UK HIGHER EDUCATION SYSTEM

A commonly told story has it that the world-famous university in Cambridge began as a Fenland refuge for scholars fleeing from the university in Oxford, after the lynching of two of their number by its townsfolk. If so, the fledgling British HE system arose in challenging times. But from this inauspicious start, it has grown and prospered. Some 800 years later, the latest Higher Education Statistics Agency (HESA) annual tables of HE include some 160 institutions, while in terms of its quality, Britain's university system is regularly rated as one of the top two globally in peer-assessed and metric-measured surveys, such as the World University Rankings produced separately by QS (Quacquarelli Symonds) and the Times Higher.

Large-scale systems, typified by the British university system, are prime targets for classification, whether from within or without, which can add order and clarity to a large and diverse array of institutions, but which is also the basis for hierarchical stratification (Croxford and Raffe 2015; Raffe and Croxford 2015; Tight 1996). One key criterion is the date when universities received degree-awarding powers. The classification here ranges from ancient foundations (such as Oxbridge, Durham and St Andrews), nineteenth-century redbricks (such as Birmingham, Bristol and Sheffield) through to the twentieth-century civics (e.g. Exeter, Leicester and Southampton) and then the 1960s plate glass institutions (such as Sussex, Essex, Lancaster and Warwick). These terms reflect different stages in the growth of the UK HE system, indicated by their architectural periodization (redbricks, plate glass) or function (those serving a particular town). The 1992 Further and Higher Education Act was a particularly important milestone in shaping the present system. It ended the previous divide between universities on the one hand and polytechnics and some colleges of HE on the other by permitting the latter to become universities.

An alternative criterion for classification, generated from within the university system, is membership of one of the self-defining mission groups, established by universities with a perceived common cause. It is in these mission groups that the hierarchy of HE becomes more apparent. The two universities in our study belong to different mission groups, UoB to the Russell Group and UWE to the University Alliance. The Russell Group is the earliest and most widely recognized such group, named after the Russell Hotel in Bloomsbury, London where their vice-chancellors first met in 1994. Today, it includes 24 larger, research-oriented UK universities. It is self-selecting (not all applications to join are successful) and is keen to differentiate its member universities from institutions offering mass HE. It sees itself, and is widely seen by those familiar with the British HE system (though not necessarily all non-member universities), as the elite tier of the UK HE hierarchy.

UWE is a member of one of the other, later, university groupings, the University Alliance. This was established in 2007, and currently embraces 19 mainly post-1992 universities (as well as Salford and the Open University) who claim a balanced portfolio of research, teaching, enterprise and innovation as integral to their missions. The University Alliance champions the work of its members as particularly focussed on applied, real-world priorities in fields such as engineering, health and design, producing job-ready graduates and potential new entrepreneurial talent, with a conscious orientation to local and regional partnerships and priorities. So the two Bristol universities are different not just in age, but in their position in a diversified and differentiated system, and this has determined whom they badge themselves alongside and form common cause with, in order, for example, to lobby Parliament about education policy.

Such university groups also have clear and self-perpetuating differentials of prestige and status, of influence and power. A widespread complaint from other universities is that the Russell Group attracts the best students and staff, and the most resources, to a disproportionate and unwarranted extent. This perpetuates and widens the differentials within the national university system. Commenting in 2015, the influential former chair of Universities UK (UUK), the committee of university vice-chancellors, envisaged a scenario whereby future UK government spending cuts and immigration controls (impacting on the recruitment of international students) would further widen these existing differentials within the HE hierarchy, by means of the Treasury asking universities to 'specialise in what they are good at' (*Times Higher*, 18 June 2015). Ominously, Jo Johnson, the Universities Minister appointed by the Conservative majority government in 2015, addressing the annual meeting of university heads two months later, told them that the future HE system only had room for high quality providers. The implication that some might fail and exit the market was supposedly a sign of healthy competition (*The Times*, 10 September 2015). Successful differentiation, it seems, may now be a matter of university life and death, not merely of status and influence.

One largely ignored feature of such national HE classifications is that, leaving aside the special case of London, the members of specific categories tend to be scattered geographically, rather than clustering in particular parts of the country. In 2015, no town or city in England contained more than one member university of any single mission group; only Birmingham (with both the University of Birmingham and Aston University) has more than one pre-1992 university, and only a handful have more than one post-1992 institution (Birmingham is again the best example). The exceptions are mostly small and specialist institutions. So as did Cambridge from Oxford in the thirteenth century, in less bloodthirsty times, 'like' universities still keep their distance one from another.

This might seem more a matter of chance than design. Whilst the pre-1992 polytechnics and colleges of HE were mainly under the regional control of Local Education Authorities, there has only very recently been any form of strategy to direct the geographical growth of the university system (Willetts 2014). Nevertheless, some spatial logic still underlies the patterning that has evolved, notwithstanding this being the aggregation of multiple, usually local and regional promotional campaigns for 'our university'. The civic pride, dreams, political clout and deep pockets of local entrepreneurs and the great and good in many nineteenth century industrial towns and cities have been key to establishing 'their' local university—for example the Frys (chocolate manufacturers) and Wills (tobacco) in Bristol, Jesse Boot of the high street chemists in Nottingham, and John Owens, a local textile merchant in Manchester. This meant that the resulting universities largely reflected the then national rank ordering of towns and cities, based on population size and significant industrial centres. As non-collegiate institutions, predating the widespread provision of halls of residence for students who were not local, they depended on securing captive markets of nearby potential students. Many had their ancestry in technically oriented institutions serving local industrial needs. On becoming universities, they also provided continuing professional education and academic outreach for those in their immediate areas, who needed this supplied *locally* if they were to be able to benefit from it at all. All this encouraged a dispersed and locally based model of university provision which, in today's more mobile, competitive and centrally funded times, has changed as universities become keen rivals in attracting recruits. Nonetheless, many students, especially adult learners, do still attend universities in their hometowns.

But the same places that had earlier promoted universities often also supported complementary institutions that maintained a technical orien-tation, again exploiting captive local markets with provision of part-time and local trade-supporting training and research. Many latterly converted, via polytechnics and Colleges of Advanced Technology (CATS), to become what are referred to as 'new' universities as a result of the 1992 Further and Higher Education Act. So the flip-side of the dispersal of '*like*' universities is that '*different*' ones often coexist as near neighbours.

The classification and stratification of the HE system outlined above is central to the research design of the *Paired Peers* project. It enabled us to compare and contrast the student experiences not just of undergraduates from different social backgrounds and studying different academic subjects, but of students attending two neighbouring universities within the same city, that are positioned differently within a hierarchical field of HE.

In the next section, we briefly sketch the historical growth of the two Bristol universities, before looking at the ways in which they now present themselves and, in particular, how these differ, leading to different reputa-tional positioning of the two universities. We then look at how reputation becomes embedded in the discourses that circulate about the two universities, and embodied in constructions of students at each institution, by looking at how participants at each university in our study articulated their understandings and perceptions of the other place, involving what Stich (2012) calls reputational affect.

TWO UNIVERSITIES: ONE CITY

The University of Bristol's ancestry can reasonably be dated to the initiative of the Headmaster of Clifton College, a leading local independent school, in 1868 (Carleton 1984). The eventual University College Bristol dates from 1876, when the new University also became the first to admit men and women on equal terms. Finance then was entirely from private sources, but government funding began in 1889, the first purpose-built site opened in 1892 and independent degree-awarding powers were awarded in 1909. Today, aside from the Veterinary School, to the rural south of the city, the main teaching and research buildings are clustered in the affluent and highly sought-after Clifton district, though intermingled with the city's other buildings rather than on a separate, exclusive campus. UoB was a founding member of the Russell Group and has recently undergone major growth as a result of increasingly relaxed government student number controls. Between 2009 and 2013, its full-time first-degree intake expanded by about 25 %, which inevitably added to pressure on the institutional and private-sector supply of student accommodation. It draws comparatively few students from the local region, and until its recent expansion housed most first-years in its own Halls of Residence through an 'accommodation guarantee', although recent expansion has seen it increasingly supplementing these with alternative, private-sector providers, sometimes in collaboration with UWE, the other university in this study. UoB is seen as exclusive in its intake, with a reputation for admitting disproportionately fewer students from under-represented social groups than its rivals, despite a large and active widening participation (WP) team, and raft of WP strategies and initiatives. The University faced severe criticism from sections of the national press and independent school sector in 2003 with allegations of naked 'social engineering' through its admissions practices, that, it was claimed, advantaged state school pupils beyond what their academic merit warranted (a charge quietly dropped a few years later).

UWE is the larger of the two Bristol universities. As noted earlier, in the academic year 2010/2011 when the *Paired Peers* cohort first arrived as students, it had over 50 % more full-time undergraduates than UoB. The two universities have some shared origins. Bristol has a maritime history, and both universities grew in part from the Navigation School of the City's Merchant Venturers (founded 1595). Both have important aerospace engineering departments linked to the South West aerospace industry (BAE, Rolls Royce and Westland). UWE can also trace its roots back to other institutions, including the Royal West of England Academy (an art education school founded in 1853), St Matthias College (teacher education, also founded in 1853), Redland College of Education (1946) and Bristol College of Commerce (1949). Bristol Polytechnic was established in 1969 with the formal merging of many of these historical antecedents. It subsequently converted to a university in 1992. Its current activities have been increasingly concentrated at a greenfield campus on the northern edge of the city (Frenchay), but there are still sizeable campuses elsewhere, in central Bristol focused on creative arts and industries, and in a suburb of Bristol and elsewhere within the region focused on health and social care. Although the Frenchay campus is green, spacious and pleasant, its surroundings are less glamorous than those occupied by UoB, which has a landmark building, the Wills Memorial Tower, dominating the landscape at the top of a major shopping street in the city.

Consistent with its local orientation in course offerings and employment opportunities, UWE's student intake has traditionally been drawn more heavily from the city and local region than UoB's. In consequence, significant provision of undergraduate residential accommodation was delayed until the last decade, but now consists of large new student villages at Frenchay, financed by UWE, and a number of joint ventures with the private sector in the city centre. Like UoB, it provides courses across a wide range of academic areas, with overlaps here between the two universities. But each has distinct offerings too, which partly reflect and reinforce the status differences between them. For example, only UWE offers nursing, architecture and fine arts, while only UoB runs degrees in medicine, veterinary science and dentistry. UWE's strong engagement with widening participation is consistent with its heavier dependence on nationally under-represented social groups within the overall undergraduate market, and, geographically, on local Bristol schools and colleges.

We turn now to evidence that brings the contemporary differences between the two universities into sharp focus. In the following tables, we summarize available data on important areas that shape the configuration and reputation of the two universities. Table 3.1 shows the profiles of the current student population, and indicates the sorts of students studying alongside the participants in the project, while Table 3.2 shows some indicators of how far the two universities have a research orientation as part of their core business.

The profile of the student population shows consistent differences in three main ways, which overall confirm that UoB has what is regularly seen as a more 'traditional' mix of students on its undergraduate courses than UWE. First, it draws more from the types of schools, geographical locations, and social strata that already produce disproportionately more

Table 3.1 Profile of student population at UWE and UoB in 2013/2014

	Measure	UoB (%)	UWE (%)
	Student background		
1.1	% intake from state schools	60	93
1.2	% intake from low participation areas	4	14
1.3	% intake from low social classes	14	30
	Type of participation and retention rates		
1.4	% mature full-time first-degree students	6	26
1.5	% part-time students	3	12
1.6	% rate of retention (i.e. non-withdrawal)	94	90
	Student origins		
1.7	% undergraduates from homes within 10 miles	4	20
1.8	% undergraduates from homes over 100 miles	51	20
1.9	% undergraduates from outside EU	12	6

Note: For full details of the variables and sources used in Tables 3.1 and 3.2 see Appendix 2.

Table 3.2 Research orientation of UWE and UoB in 2013/2014

	Measure	UoB (%)	UWE (%)
	Research personnel		
2.1	Postgraduates as % of total students	26	13
	Research quality assessment		
2.2	REF 2014 Grade point average	3.2	2.7
2.3	REF 2014 Research intensity	2.3	0.8
	Research income streams		
2.4	% Research in HEFCE grant	61	36

HE students (1.1–1.3). Second, it concentrates relatively more on 'young' participants in HE, that is, students who have just left school or maybe had a gap year, rather than mature students, possibly with existing family commitments and work experience (1.4), and most are studying full-time (1.5). UoB students are, perhaps because they are mainly young participants, more likely to complete their courses rather than to withdraw before the end (1.6). Finally, far fewer students at UoB are from the local area (1.7, 1.8) and there are more international students from beyond the EU, who do not qualify to pay the 'home' fees charged to all UK and EU-based students (1.9). Here, overall, we see evidence of an elite Russell Group university concentrating on full-time undergraduate programmes, tapping into well-established market segments in the UK of mainly young full-time students, as well as attracting international students for whom university status and prestige can be paramount. UWE, in contrast, actively pursues locally focused widening participation strategies as part of its core business, and has a flexibility of course provision to match.

Regarding research orientation, UoB scores more highly on research indicators across the board, as shown in Table 3.2. As the table shows, the indicators include the higher number of post-graduate students, UoB's superior performance in the 2014 UK-wide Research Excellence Framework (REF) assessment of academic staff and the greater award of research income.

Easily available public data on the post-university experiences of students from the two universities are more elusive. However, the recent analysis of the Great British Class Survey shows that the two Bristol universities are distinctive one from another in a similar way to other same-city pairs of old and new universities (Savage et al. 2015). Of those Bristol graduates now aged between 35 and 50 who completed the survey, those from UoB were over twice as likely as their UWE equivalents to be classified as being members of the 'elite' compared to the 'established middle class' or neither of these, in the new class classification the Savage research team developed.

All these factors contribute not just to the particular environment of each university, but to their different reputations. The first part of this chapter has shown how reputation is built up historically. But reputation is also historically and socially situated, with the markers of prestige at a given time a means of positioning within the field of HE. So, for example, research assumes a higher importance than teaching in the prestige attached to UK universities at the present time, though there are attempts by the UK government's Department for Business, Innovation and Skills to increase the importance attached to teaching through a new Teaching Excellence Framework (BIS 2015). Reputational positioning by institutions then plays out in the lives and experience of students, and in the ways that students view their own positioning in the field of HE as a result of the university they attend. Reputation therefore does not just have tangible effects; it creates reputational *affects* (Stich 2012).

Reputation and Reputational Affect

In what follows, we explore how the reputational differences between the two universities in our study, resulting from the markers of prestige and positioning outlined earlier, become ingrained in students, in the form of 'reputational affects' (Stich 2012, p. 30). In a study of social class and HE in the USA, Stich defines reputational affects as follows:

> Reputational affects are the deeply felt, socially constructed components of everyday life—they are the more sticky residues left behind by constancy of reputation than reputation itself—the stuff that leaves a lasting mark and won't wash clean or easily shake free. (Stich 2012, p. 30)

These reputational *affects* are less quantifiable than the more tangible *effects*, particularly of attending a university with a prestigious reputation, but they are deeply felt, and they leave a lasting mark in the sense that graduates will be viewed in light of where they graduated from, and see themselves in that light. These affects work their way into the discourses of students, and contribute to the shaping of students' dispositions. The affects of reputation can be elusive and articulated as a sense of something not quite tangible (Stich 2012). We found that they were often most clearly articulated relationally—we learned much about reputational affect, by asking participants in the project about the differences between the students and the university that they were attending, and the 'other place'. It was the accumulation of small comments, perceptions and observations amongst the participants in our study that built up a sense of how institutional reputation and positioning creates affects in the lives of both working-class and middle-class students.

In her work, Stich focuses on the affects accumulated through attending a low-ranking institution in the USA, and how these work through into the habitus of working-class students, contributing to the reproduction of inequalities. Here, we consider reputational affects in relation to both working-class and middle-class students. While the students in our study were attending two differently positioned universities, neither is a low-ranking institution and both have good reputations. Yet, as this chapter shows, reputations are constructed relationally, structuring the perceived opportunities and limits of each university, so that UWE's reputational position is constructed in relation to universities like UoB, which is a higher ranking institution in the HE field. Reputational affects can then be seen in the construction of boundaries, that are both social and physical, so that even though they live and study in the same city, students from the two universities in our study led largely separate lives, consistent with a classed conceptualization of each university's milieu. We found that a small number of students transgressed these boundaries. This occurred particularly where individual working-class participants felt themselves to be out of place in the very middle-class milieu of the University of Bristol, while some students from established middle-class backgrounds felt like 'a fish out of water' at UWE, the modern post-92 university.

Student Contact with the 'Other Place'

Although their main campuses are some distance apart, being located in the same city means that UoB and UWE students potentially have many opportunities for mutual interaction, for example, as near neighbours in popular student residential areas, through sharing leisure and extra-curricular pursuits, and taking part-time employment in the city's shops, pubs and restaurants. There are many bars, nightclubs and other venues in the city, where students may meet, while private student accommodation providers offer spaces for both sets of students.

However, what became apparent in the interviews with participants in the *Paired Peers* project is the ways in which there were both social and physical boundaries between students attending the two universities. The following two tables show levels of contact between students at each university (Table 3.3) and perceived differences between the universities and their students (Table 3.4), as reported by participants during their third year of study.

As Table 3.3 indicates, students reported limited contact with students from the other university. The geographical location of UWE's main campus, on the edge of the Bristol urban area and just outside the city boundary, placed it beyond the horizons of most UoB students. Carly

Table 3.3   Levels of contact between students at UoB and UWE

Level of contact	UoB (%)		UWE (%)	
	Working-class	Middle-class	Working-class	Middle-class
None or almost none	61	58	91	36
Occasional and usually of just one type of contact	22	32	9	50
Substantial and usually of more than one type of contact	17	10	0	14
All respondents coded (n = 62)	100 (n = 18)	100 (n = 19)	100 (n = 11)	100 (n = 14)

Table 3.4   Perceived differences between UWE and UoB

Perceived difference	UoB (%)		UWE (%)	
	Working-class	Middle-class	Working-class	Middle-class
No opinion offered	22	10	36	31
Modest differences, usually of just one type of difference and often prompted	50	30	45	19
Significant differences, usually of more than one type, and usually spontaneous	28	60	18	50
All respondents coded (n = 65)	100 (n = 18)	100 (n = 20)	100 (n = 11)	100 (n = 16)

(UoB, working-class) admitted she had no idea where UWE was, and quite possibly others had not either, while Sally (UoB, middle-class) commented about UWE: '*it's in the middle of nowhere*'. UoB, in contrast, is centrally located, and many of the clubs, restaurants, and shops providing work, leisure and accommodation for students from both universities are close to where UoB is situated. For instance, one nightclub that hosts nights for UWE students is in Clifton, much closer to the main UoB campus than it is to UWE. Moreover, some of the UWE middle-class respondents, especially those from the upper fractions of the middle-class, had deliberately chosen to live in Clifton and other parts of town where they were primarily amongst UoB students.

Nevertheless, although they reported little contact, the majority of respondents offered views about the differences between the two universities, as shown in Table 3.4, with middle-class students from each university having stronger views of the differences than their working-class peers. Sometimes these accounts of differences arose spontaneously from the flow of the conversation between student and their interviewer, but at other times interviewers had to prompt their respondents to add illustrative detail to their initial opinion that the two sets of Bristol students were indeed different, explaining what these differences might be.

Although participants almost always prefaced their comments by admitting a tendency to stereotype, and said they personally disagreed with the stereotype, the reputation and positioning of the two universities were nevertheless very much 'in the heads' of the students in our study.

Constructing the Classed Reputations of UWE and UoB

Reputation was produced and reproduced through a constant circulation and telling and retelling of stories from student to student, through social media posts and artefacts, as well as behaviours—we heard, for example, the (maybe apocryphal) story of UoB students goading those from UWE by waving money at them when spectating at inter-university 'Varsity' events. Even though UWE became a university more than 20 years ago in 1992, when the participants in this project were only one or two years old, it was still referred to in interviews as the 'polytechnic' in contrast to the 'redbrick', 'Russell Group' University of Bristol (e.g. by Marcus, UoB working-class; Harriet, UWE middle-class; Oscar, UWE middle-class). This clearly named status divide was given added impetus by the slogan on a T-shirt on sale for UoB students, which read: *100 % cotton, 0 % poly* (Fig. 3.1). The reputational affect of UoB is clearly underscored by the comment '*Who said it's the taking part that counts?*' beneath the image, a smug indication of the awareness that the value of participation in HE can be enhanced or diminished by the type of institution attended.

Institutional status was then seen to create a differently classed milieu at each university, particularly an environment of middle-class privilege at UoB. Cerys (UoB, middle-class) described UoB students as '*London-based posh people*', while Nicole (UoB, working-class) explained: '*It is obviously like a very posh redbrick university* [...] *The whole public school, quite posh, a little bit elitist, I would say that I see that quite a lot.*' UWE students similarly associated UoB students with the privileged middle-classes. Lloyd, a UWE student who was himself middle-class, said: '*I kind of see them as having this life set up ahead of them, this amazing rich and wealthy life*'. Kyle, a UWE student from a working-class background, said of UoB students:

Fig. 3.1 University of Bristol 'varsity' T-shirt

You'd probably expect them to be in the Rowing Club, or in Polo or something, wearing their Ralph Lauren, or their Hollister probably.

As Kyle's comment indicates, university classed differences were made visible in students' dress. Rose, a middle-class student at UoB, talked about the 'rahs' at UoB, who were defined by the way they dressed:

R: Well Bristol uni is just full of rahs. Like, it's so tiring.

I: For the purpose of the recorder explain to me what a rah is.

R: Sort of upper middle-class person who probably went to private school, wears like red corduroy pants and flip-flops and a gilet.

I: A what?

R: A gilet. That's how I would describe a rah. [...] Bristol's quite something. You can tell who are the Bristol students, like on a night out the Bristol students are the ones that will have made it look as though they have not made an effort but they've spent like hours getting ready. [...] When I go out I like to dress up and put on a nice dress and stuff but if you wear heels here it's like, you're shunned if you wear heels. And you can't make it look as though you've made an effort.

Classed differences were also apparent in demeanour. Garry, a working-class student at UoB, suggested that '*Bristol students have a reputation for being a bit arrogant*' and Connie, also UoB working-class, gave an example of her experience of this in her part-time waitressing job:

Some students [from UoB] can come in and they do live up to the stereotype and they are really fussy and difficult. I see it when I'm like serving, like some people who are ... I mean it's not necessarily bad, I mean they're not doing anything wrong, it's just like "I want this without this and this and this" and it just makes it a little bit…and like complaining that their food is like two minutes late.

The UWE milieu was defined in contrast to the middle-class privilege of UoB as '*a lot less upper middle-class*' (Elliott, UoB, middle-class). Garry (UoB, working-class), who commented above on UoB students' reputation for arrogance, suggested that '*there is more of a humility to UWE students, they tend to be more down to earth maybe about certain things.*'

Zoe, also working-class and studying at UoB, described the difference in the dress and demeanour of UWE students, and how, as a working-class student, she felt more at home with UWE students, who were 'normal' and dressed 'up' in the same way as her:

> To be honest the vast majority of UWE students I've met I get on better with, maybe I'd fit in better there anyway. Like the girls are, you know, they're normal girls. Like they'll dress up when they're out, they wear heels, they sort of have a laugh and a joke and a giggle and they seem to be sort of normal and nice in a way, more rounded as people, not entitled and arrogant. The girls in Bristol they won't wear heels, so I go out and everyone looks at me like "Who is this slut?" Do you know what I mean?

These perceptions of classed ways of being and doing ran alongside a sense of academic dissimilarities between the students at the two universities, so that class and academic differences elided together. This involved perceptions of academic rigour, and a view that students at each university were more or less academic. Anna, a working-class student at UoB, described UWE as offering more applied subjects '*more businessy and teacher training and stuff*' meaning that it was '*less academically rigorous*' whereas '*Bristol students are more sort of academic*', while Adele, a working-class student at UWE, offered the following perceptions of UoB students:

> I think there's a general kind of feeling amongst UWE students that…they [UoB students] are generally brighter. Let's be honest, most of the people here if we had the grades we'd probably be there, but we can't so we're here.

Being 'brighter' and more 'academic' were therefore associated with being middle-class and studying at UoB, even when students sought to stand back from fully agreeing with what they described, as indicated in comments by Martin and Scarlett (both UoB, middle-class):

> There's the obviously kind of clichéd dichotomy between the Bristol student as very middle-class and very intellectual and well educated, and the UWE student being working-class and not as intelligent. But do I think that's true? Kind of. I think definitely there's like a demographic difference between the two universities, but like on a real individual level I don't think there is much difference because, I don't know, I think if I went to UWE I don't think I'd be that different, or like I don't think I intuitively seem "Bristol Uni". (Martin, UoB, middle-class)

We do have a slight rivalry with UWE, you know, we're the posh lot and they're the fairly normal lot who, I guess, take slightly less academic subjects for some things, but equally we know that they're far better, like their departments are a lot better in some things than ours are. I don't know, I wouldn't say that we were that different particularly, we're all just uni students I guess. (Scarlett, UoB, middle-class)

But despite the suggestion that 'we're all just uni students', the differences outlined above were also seen to construct differences in attitudes to learning, and entitlement in relation to academic knowledge (Reay et al. 2010). UoB students were defined as hard working, with the right attitudes to learning, and the ability to engage with academic knowledge. Max (UoB, middle-class) explained:

There's kind of a certain set of the student body who feel like "well I'm at this university, I've done really well to get here, I've had to get really good grades, I'm really lucky to be here, I need to do well academically otherwise it's just a waste, and I need to make the most of what they're giving me". So that kind of informs certain behaviour.

Marcus (UoB, working-class) contrasted UoB and UWE students as follows:

Bristol […] is more a place where you are those people who grasp the academic part of a subject quite easily; and UWE, the style of learning is slightly different, and I might say more supported learning, I don't know why. I think here at Bristol you could get chucked a lot of information and interpret it for yourself. I think at UWE a lot more is expanded upon and explained.

The learner identities of UWE students, as the above comments suggest, were perceived as dissimilar. Max (UoB, middle-class) commented about UWE students:

I think there is a sense amongst Bristol students, that UWE is either less prestigious or less academic, or whatever, that it attracts a certain type of person who perhaps doesn't take their studies as seriously or whatever.

Bianca, Martha and Garry, also UoB students, offered anecdotal examples that helped to underline this perception:

I know some people [friends from home] who don't do work and just kind of skim by, they're the ones who go to Portsmouth [described as similar to UWE], whereas everyone I know at Bristol does generally put in more effort. (Bianca, UoB, working-class)

I think a lot of my friends from UWE are people who are really intelligent but who haven't necessarily like worked really hard the whole way through school, they've done like different things, they've had fun or kind of had other focuses. (Martha, UoB, middle-class)

Bristol students have a reputation of being more studious I'd say, definitely. And there might be some truth to that, even though I've sort of listed exceptions. A lot of my home friends will still be going on nights out and stuff like that during the exam period, and that would be inconceivable to a lot from Bristol—no, that wouldn't happen. (Garry, UoB, working-class)

Students at UWE offered similar perceptions of the difference between UWE and UoB students:

I think UoB students see the opportunities more, you know the opportunities that are open to them and the possibilities of what they can do, more than UWE students. [...] Generally you'd say they see a broader prospective of what they can do, you know with hard work kind of thing. (Dylan, UWE, middle-class)

I get the idea that they're more studious, and that's probably completely wrong, but more like Oxford and Cambridge, that they do more work and socialise less, but that's probably not true. And UWE is more for socializing. (Sophie, UWE, working-class)

'Knowing' all these differences as classed differences was particularly apparent amongst students who described how they or their friends felt like fish out of water in the milieu of one or the other university. Freya and Zoe, working-class students at UoB, described not fitting in at their university. Zoe, quoted earlier in this chapter, described how she felt she would fit in better with UWE students than she did at UoB, and Freya explained:

I fit in at Langford [one of the UoB campuses], which is where all my lectures are, but I still feel kind of uneasy in the main campus, I don't know why. (Freya, UoB, working-class)

Jasmine (UWE, working-class) described how a friend had dropped out of UoB, because: '*she hated it, she didn't fit in at all, everyone on her course was called Claudia and had daddies and ponies, yeah, stuck up.*' This sense of discomfort was also felt by a number of middle-class students at UWE, who sought to overcome this by spending their time with UoB students. Dylan (UWE, middle-class) chose to live in private halls of residence with UoB students. Francesca (UWE, middle-class) also spent her time with UoB students, living in Clifton, a part of the city where many UoB students lived, and going out on 'Bristol Uni nights'. She felt that she stood out at UWE and had found it difficult to fit in:

I: OK, and how well do you feel that you fit in at UWE?

F: Definitely when I started and into my second year I don't think I did— again this is like stereotypes as an overall picture of UWE. Firstly because none of my friends or family had gone to like an ex-Poly, so I guess I sort of stood out—not stood out but it's different. So already you start thinking "I don't know if I'm going to fit here." I guess that's what I thought. Third year a bit less, I felt that I actually fit in a bit more.

Hannah (UoB, middle-class) offered a similar story of how a friend studying at UWE had had to work hard to find people she felt comfortable with, eventually finding friends through the Sailing Society—an activity still considered 'deeply middle-class' (Wallop 2013):

My friend [who is at UWE], she was quite unhappy in her flat because she found the girls in her flat were just very different to her and like, you know, when I was describing the typical student, she said that they went out drinking all the time and the most important thing to them was like getting dressed up for a night out. That could so easily just be her flat and I know there's loads of people at UWE that probably aren't like that. She's managed to find a really nice group of friends but she's found them all through the Sailing Society. (Hannah, UoB, middle-class)

While it is in feelings of being out of place and other that deeply felt reputational affects are most clearly articulated, there is a wider narrative communicated in students' perceptions of each other and of themselves that marks out differences between UWE and UoB. In this narrative, UWE students are intellectually inferior to students positioned in universities of higher rank and reputation, such as UoB, they are party people, less well prepared for HE study, more suited to vocational subjects, and they are more working-class. This narrative gathers momentum and becomes a naturalized account of reality. As Stich observes: 'reputation acquires a certain durability over time, retains its value, and outlasts realities that exist outside of its construction' (Stich 2012, p. 107). What is less clearly named is the sort of resources and capitals available to certain students, that allow them to fit seamlessly into university study, with a sense of confidence and entitlement about their place in HE. It is this that we go on to explore in more detail in the next four chapters.

Concluding Comments

This chapter has outlined the history of Bristol's two universities, and the socially and historically situated nature of their positioning in a hierarchically stratified field of HE in the UK. We have considered how the reputational positioning of the two universities feeds into what Reay et al. (2010, p. 3) refer to as the 'expressive order' of institutions, embodied in the collectivity of students: 'in their dress, demeanour and attitudes, in particular their attitudes towards learning and their degree of confidence and entitlement in relation to academic knowledge'. This embodiment of the expressive order creates what Stich (2012) calls reputational affects. We have shown how a classed sense of entitlement amongst middle-class students can lead to disappointment and discomfort for some of those from middle-class backgrounds studying at a modern, post-1992 university, while for working-class students, notions of being 'normal' and 'ordinary' (Roberts 2010, p. 12) continue to have lasting weight, particularly for those attending the elite University of Bristol.

CHAPTER 4

Getting In

It's just a standard thing for my school, everyone went to uni. And then my parents both went to uni, both my sisters went to uni, so it's just kind of a standard thing that I would go to university as well. It was one of those things that everyone did their UCAS application, everyone just went to uni. (Joel, middle-class, UWE)

I didn't know if I should be reading or anything beforehand. No-one in my family had really been to university before and I was like "I don't know what to do". It was really strange. But it's fine. You get used to it. (Abigail, working-class, UWE)

INTRODUCTION

The young people participating in the *Paired Peers* study entered university in the autumn of 2010. Although there was by then a new Conservative-Liberal Democrat Coalition government in the UK, they began university at the point when the previous Labour Government's goal of 50 % participation in some form of higher education (HE) amongst 18–30-year olds was to have been achieved. Although this ambitious target for participation was narrowly missed, with 47 % of young people in England going into HE that year (BIS 2012), the figure still marked a significant increase from a generation previously—just 18 % went to HE in 1988, for instance (Chowdry et al. 2010).

However, overall figures for participation in HE mask significant differences, particularly with respect to social class, in terms of who goes to

© The Editor(s) (if applicable) and The Author(s) 2016
A.M. Bathmaker et al., *Higher Education, Social Class and Social Mobility*, DOI 10.1057/978-1-137-53481-1_4

university and to which type of university they go. The social make-up of the UK undergraduate intake in 2010, the year our study began, is shown in Table 1.1 in Chapter 1, along with numbers for the two universities in our study for the same period. There are significant differences between Bristol's two universities in terms of the class background of new undergraduates starting in 2010 and also between each of the universities and the wider UK undergraduate intake for the year. Both universities in our study have levels of middle-class students above the national average, particularly UoB.

This chapter is the first of four chapters focusing in detail on the experience of students in the *Paired Peers* study. We look here at their routes into university, including the extent to which it was either a *hope* or an *expectation*, and at the role of families and schools in the process. While previous research has looked at equity and inequalities in access to HE (e.g. Adnett et al. 2011; Boliver 2011; Jones 2013; Zimdars et al. 2009), and at the ways in which structuring factors such as institutional habitus affect decision-making and 'choice' (Reay et al. 2005), here, we focus on the ways in which progression to HE was a planned part of the lives of participants in the *Paired Peers* study. While HE appeared to be a taken-for-granted part of the middle-class life course, assumed and expected from an early age, for working-class students planning occurred at a later stage, with HE only becoming part of horizons for action (Hodkinson and Sparkes 1997) as young people reached the later stages of secondary education.

In this chapter, we differentiate between students who were determined planners and those whose plans were more open-ended. We also discuss reasons for the decision about which university to attend, and we draw attention to classed dimensions of the routes into HE study. Working-class young people have lower chances than the middle-classes of getting into university, especially the more prestigious institutions like UoB. Therefore, the working-class undergraduates in our study must be seen as having made it against the odds, at both UWE and UoB. This means a harder furrow to plough than for their middle-class counterparts, and is indicative in many cases of qualities of perseverance and grit.

WHY GO TO UNIVERSITY?

The notion of a 'graduate premium' underpins the policies governing the funding of HE in the UK, justifying the shift in financial burden from the public purse through general taxation to the individual through the system of student loans. The graduate premium, and the expectation that being a graduate would lead to enhanced prospects, was particularly important to working-class participants in the project. Shane for instance (working-class, UWE) referred to graduates having 'better job prospects' and Anna (working-class, UoB) explained that her reason for going to HE was the difficulty of earning much without a degree:

> Well the main reason I think is because I wanted to get a better job. I mean there's no middle brackets for people who have A Levels, there's no job market just for A Levels, so it's kind of…you've got a very low wage I think when you start and it's really hard to then progress and get a good wage.

In other working-class students' accounts there was a theme of escape from an area which only offered negatives to them, as in Zoe's statement of why she chose to go to university:

> Because I had the ability to do it and I didn't want to waste my potential. I'm from, not a deprived area, but from an area where I see a lot of deprivation and I see the loons just wandering around jobless, and I didn't want to fall into that bracket. There's no big opportunities and I've always felt like I was meant for bigger things regardless of what they were, and so I thought I can do this, I may as well utilize whatever I've got and just go to university and get a degree, even though I'm not necessarily an academic person.

Although good careers also figured in responses from middle-class participants, their comments suggested that they had the luxury of additionally using university study as a rite of passage to adulthood. Dylan (middle-class, UWE) explained:

> I think, as much as it is the degree, you get a lot more from it besides that, like the life skills, just down to things like living on your own, like sorting yourself out, even things down to shopping. When you live at home you don't have any grasp on planning, like any planning whatsoever, so I now think you get general skills for life, like social skills, talking to people that you might not have met, you might not like, but learning to deal with those…it just builds you as a person as a whole rather than just for the degree, rather than just like education, it's more than that, it's everything, it shapes you socially.

Harriet (middle-class, UWE) also spoke of university allowing her to 'meet so many different people', and suggested an additional benefit that resonated with the responses of several other participants. It offered the opportunity to delay decision-making about longer-term career goals. These comments fit with Brake's (1980) view of university as a 'moratorium' between adolescence and adulthood for middle-class young people, a time to grow up and learn about the possibilities for the adult self.

For some participants including Carly (middle-class, UoB), going to university was simply what people like her *do*. Bourdieu would refer to this as her middle-class habitus, the 'taken-for-granted' or 'common sense' way of being:

> It sounds weird but I never thought of doing anything other than going to university. I think for most people in my school, it's more or less the standard thing to do. Like you go to high school, you go to sixth form, you go to university. I wasn't like forced into it, it's just what happens.

For students like Carly, the 'decision' to go to university was hardly a decision at all. As she explained, it was something that just happened, it barely required any thought. Here, we can discern the power of the habitus to direct thinking and action so that choices are made at an almost intuitive rather than conscious level. We explore this notion further in the following sections. Parental and familial influence are integral to the structuring of the young people's habitus. They channel their attitudes to and thinking about HE both directly and indirectly.

Decision-Making: The Influence of Parents and Family

Students' accounts revealed how the role of families was central to the choices of the young people in the study, with parents being particularly important. Sebastian (middle-class, UoB) told of how his parents were both the first in their own families to go to university, and that for his generation, there was an expectation that they would do the same. This expectation was fairly common amongst our middle-class respondents, sometimes explicitly stated by parents and sometimes an unspoken expectation.

This was in contrast to some of the working-class participants. Unlike Sebastian's university-educated parents, no one in Jackie's family (working-class, UoB) had been to university—she described herself as 'the first person to test it out'. Jackie told us how her mother had helped her decide which university to go to and what subject to study, but in the same sort of way her mother would help her with any significant decision she had to make; she could not draw on personal experience of university to help. Her mother's practical advice tended to focus on independent living, such as what Jackie should take away to university with her, and to reassure her that her father could always come and pick her up if she needed to return home at short notice. Like other working-class students in particular, Jackie's parents ideally wanted her to be studying relatively close to the family home.

Other working-class parents took a more *laissez faire* approach to the decision-making process, not because they did not care, but because they knew they had little expertise upon which they could draw. For instance Sean's mother (working-class, UoB) simply said: 'whatever university you want to go to and course, whichever interests you'. Garry spoke of how his mother could not offer him guidance:

> Because obviously she didn't go to university herself or never went through that sort of application process so I think she sort of felt…she didn't really know too much about it herself so, I guess she didn't know what she could contribute in a sense of what to do, what course to do and whatever.

While parents like Sean's and Garry's were supportive of their children's choices they could not necessarily be influential in terms of the decision-making process; this may explain why working-class students may develop skills of self-reliance and resilience that aid their progress through university. Needing to take charge of their own direction without falling back on family expectations or parental guidance, these students have to develop an orientation towards thinking outside of the family habitus (Reay 1998).

An older sibling who had attended university could be an alternative source of advice, encouragement and inspiration for students whose parents did not have the cultural resources gained from attending university themselves to provide advice and help. Adele (working-class, UWE) was one such student. She remembered visiting her older sister at university and how:

> She'd have a new social group of friends, she was loving it, and she was the one who was always pushing me "you need to go to uni, you're bright, you need to go to uni".

Kyle (working-class, UWE) similarly recalled how much his brother had enjoyed being a student:

After he did his [degree], he was like "you've got to do it!" I didn't think I could go through this life without going to uni because it is such an amazing experience—and it is.

As these comments indicate, with siblings attending university the idea of HE can become part of a young person's horizons for action, and something to be considered, especially when siblings offer active encouragement. However, this is quite different from the taken-for-granted family expectations of the middle-classes. Here, students have to make a conscious decision rather than following an expected, almost predestined pathway.

Decision-Making: The Influence of School

School also played a key role in participants' decision-making. When students, especially those middle-class respondents who had gone to selective or private, fee-paying schools, had attended schools where the majority of pupils progressed to HE, there was a strong emphasis on getting pupils into high-ranking universities. Grace, a middle-class student from UoB, had attended a selective sixth form college that had the reputation of being one of the best nationally. The expectation was that everyone would apply to university. There were additional systems in place providing support to those applying to Oxbridge, which Grace had been encouraged to do, though she decided against it. She explained:

They were really good. They had loads of helping tutorials and things. And we had help filling in our UCAS forms, and the Oxbridge people had ... they all had their own Oxbridge person to help them with all that. Everyone had to have two careers interviews. And my English teacher helped me write my personal statement.

Adrian (middle-class, UoB) attended a high-achieving state school that also encouraged students they thought were high achievers to apply to 'good', high-ranking universities:

I was coming from an environment where my parents had always made sure that I worked hard in school and I think that the teachers there were very keen to get the kids that they thought could get into the good universities into them. They put a lot of effort into helping us with our applications to university. I think that they cared a lot more because they knew they had to work harder for us to get us in I think. So most students, there was a focus on getting pass rates but I think the students that they did think could get grades above that they really did work hard for.

In the cases above, aspiring to go to university was a given, and the schools could concentrate their efforts on maximizing the number of young people gaining a place at high-ranking institutions.

In contrast, Adele (working-class UWE) told us how expectations at her school and amongst her contemporaries were markedly different to those facing Grace and Adrian:

> A vast majority of people I went to high school with didn't go to uni, and to be honest that wasn't on their radar as it wasn't done. That wasn't part of what they grew up with, their parents didn't go to uni. I think a lot of people, especially now that I've come to uni, it's expected, whereas where I come from it isn't really expected, it's more "oh, you're going to uni?" It's not "yeah of course I'm going to uni" that's what's expected. It was more you have a job, boring, manual 9 to 5 job and that was it, and you maybe have a relationship, you settle down and you earn. That's just boring, I don't want to do that, but the vast majority of people did do that. A number of my friends from back home have got babies now, and not necessarily all of them are with their partners. And to them, that's fine and they can deal with it and they're happy, but to me it would be like living in a prison, I couldn't do that at all.

Adele's cultural milieu did not foster an automatic expectation or entitlement to progress smoothly from sixth form or college to university. For her contemporaries, university was not part of what was thinkable; the conception was not part of their habitus. Her choice to study was in many ways against-the-grain. Like many other working-class people before her, Adele used a desire for what she thought would be a better life to drive her on towards university, and, as we discuss in Chapter 5, this drive and determination, and the resilience it fosters, helped some disadvantaged students like Adele to achieve success in HE.

Choice of University

As well as influences on their decision to go to university, we asked participants their reasons for choosing to study in Bristol, at UWE or UoB. Outcomes at advanced level played a significant part in which university students attended. Students were very aware of the status and hierarchies of universities. Institutions such as the University of Bristol, with more demanding entry requirements in terms of UCAS tariffs or A Level grades were viewed as being of a higher standard, and the entry grades were seen to represent the quality of the HEI.

However, the way students acted on this information varied. Middle-class students tended to display attitudes of entitlement to go to higher ranked institutions, and did all they could to qualify in terms of grades, offers and UCAS applications. With help from schools and parents they knew how to 'play the game'. On occasion, this involved taking a chance on getting a place at a Russell Group university. Harry, (middle-class, UoB) progressed to UoB instead of going to Aberystwyth University, because he included UoB on his choice form as an outside chance, indicating a tacit knowledge of how to play the 'educational game'. Others, particularly those from the upper fractions of the middle-classes, described how they had not achieved the hoped-for grades at advanced level, and had had to 'trade down' in terms of university status. These included Francesca, Nicholas and Oscar, who are discussed in detail later in this chapter, and Amber, who admitted:

> I only decided I was going to come here a week before I actually came, I didn't really have many expectations of UWE. I didn't get the grades to go to any of my choices. Warwick was my first choice. I came through clearing and got in here.

Some working-class students also had aspirations based on their understanding of the hierarchy, such as Zoe, a working-class law student at UoB, who told us that her law degree would be worth more in the job market than one from UWE, but others seemed to accept that they would achieve lower grades at advanced level and that a lower-ranked university might be more suitable for them; a kind of 'knowing their place' that mirrored their class habitus.

Moreover, when working-class students had considered or been encouraged to apply to the most prestigious universities of Oxford or Cambridge, the interview process could simply serve to confirm that they would be a fish out of water at these universities. Megan (working-class, UoB), studying English, explained:

> I didn't know that I was good at school until I got to secondary school and then I realized that I was actually getting really good grades, and so I

decided that I really wanted to go to uni, I really liked learning [...]. And so I did really well at GCSE and I was like "oh that's really cool". Did really well at AS and I thought "cor that's brilliant". And then as soon as I got to A level and someone put a mark on it, it was like "you have to get 3 As if you want to move on", that was like ... ultimate crash. So I just had a complete panic year with A level. But then applied to uni, applied to Oxford, Bristol, Warwick, Durham and Exeter. And then I got interviewed at Oxford, had a horrible time and really, really didn't enjoy it there at all. Just because I had a really horrible interview, I didn't get on with anyone and I spent the entire time sat in my room thinking "oh my God". I was there 2 days and I was like "I can't speak any more". So that really ... like up until that point all my teachers had been telling me, you know, "you'll go to Oxford" which is like a rare thing from a state school, a college, there would only be 2 people out of 600 a year who go.

A number of working-class students in particular had chosen to stay and study locally, where they would continue to be near to friends from home. These included Garry, who grew up in the east of the city. He and his friends who progressed to HE generally went on to institutions in the local region:

A lot of them [study] locally, I've got friends who are at UWE actually. Quite a few went to Bath Spa, a couple went to Bath and two others to Bristol so mainly locally. There's a few that have gone further afield. Three of my friends went to Cardiff, well one to Cardiff and two to, I think it's UWIC, another one there and another one went to Sheffield, but mainly local universities it seems. So I thought, you know, "do the same, stay in the area". (Garry, working-class, UoB)

Travelling in Hope or Expectation?

When first interviewing the students, we were struck by the often stark differences in their approach to making decisions about going to university as the quotes from Abigail and Joel which opened this chapter illustrate. The accounts offered in the first interview frequently demonstrated class-based differences between students on the basis of whether they had *hoped* or *expected* to go to university. These tendencies were often suggested to be the consequence of the influence of 'significant others' within their lives—family members, staff at the school they had attended, or their peer groups, or, in many cases, a combination of these.

62   A.M. BATHMAKER ET AL.

Working-Class Hopes of Going to University: The Chance Parents Didn't Have

Without an expectation of university built in through family and schooling experiences the decision to go to university for working-class students is not taken lightly. As university is not part of an inter-generational family history or tradition, decision-making about going to university becomes more complex. It involves thinking through the reasons for choosing further study, and justifying their decisions with recourse to articulating the planned direction of their lives and their future.

Justin (working-class, UoB) explained how it was mid-way through his secondary school when he began to hope to go to university. He suggested, '*I was always academic as opposed to vocational, so for me university was the next step*'. His aspirations were reinforced when his A Level results came out: '*well obviously I got quite good grades, so I figured "don't let them go to waste but take them further"*'. Justin arrived at his decision to go to university by taking incremental steps towards HE as opposed to having an internalized view of HE always on his horizon.

Anna (working-class, UoB) also spoke of how her decision to go to university evolved gradually, taking the chance to succeed that her parents never had:

> I don't think I'd be here if it wasn't for my parents. [...] They didn't really get to succeed themselves. And it's quite strange because you come to university and you see everybody ... their parents in careers, and you think that they've grown up always hearing about going to university and getting a degree. I didn't grow up hearing any of that, I just kind of ... it came to me in the sixth form that maybe that's what I would do. I was quite different to everybody else.

Where working-class students were encouraged by their school or college, as was the case with Connie, studying drama at UoB, the encouragement was not necessarily focused just on university:

> It was really encouraged in the sixth form college that we pursue higher education, whether it was a course at college or university, or some sort of internship or apprenticeship.

But as a further comment she made suggested, she had a tacit understanding that university was the 'best' choice: '*I knew that I wanted to go to university and further my education, really sort of get as much as I can out of my education while I can.*'

A challenge here is that students may preclude themselves from future pathways, by choosing or not choosing to study particular subjects through to advanced level. Leo, studying economics at UWE, did not have the qualifications he needed to go to the University of Bristol, or to study the subject he would have preferred (engineering), because he had avoided taking maths at A level, and was not advised that this would limit his future opportunities:

Leo: I wanted to go to the University of Bristol but they wouldn't take me.

Interviewer: Oh, is that because of the grades or just because of lack of places?

Leo: No it's because I didn't take Maths, they wanted Maths and I didn't do it for A level. I'd rather have done an Engineering course, but you needed Maths for that, so I couldn't follow up for that.

Interviewer: Did they not do Maths at your college?

Leo: Yeah they did but I didn't really like it when I went from school, so I just thought, they can use Physics A level.

For all of these students, university was not 'just what happens', to echo their middle-class counterpart Carly, referred to earlier, it was what they made happen through their own hopes and dreams. University was something they hoped for rather than something to which they assumed entitlement, and this required them to take active steps to progress to HE study.

Middle-Class Expectations of Going to University: 'What We Do in Our Family'

In contrast, the majority of the middle-class students, particularly those from upper fractions of the middle-classes and those who had attended private schools, had always assumed they would be going to university. Their parents and wider families had gone to university and going to university was an unquestioned part of a normalized educational pathway. For them, the only meaningful questions were which university to choose and what they would study there.

Grace (UoB) suggested 'I think I just always kind of assumed that I'd go school, A Levels, uni', and for Farrah (UoB) it was 'the obvious thing, "you're definitely going to university", that wasn't a question as such'.

Lilly's (UWE) response further demonstrates the importance of familial habitus. She said:

> I think probably the main reason was because it was expected of me, because both my parents went to uni and my grandparents went to university as well, so it's just what we do in our family.

Rose (UoB) similarly commented 'I guess it had always just been expected that I would go to university', and for Francesca (UWE), it was also wholly expected within her family: 'Everyone in my family's done it and they've all enjoyed it and I wanted to do it.' For Harry (UoB) it was taken-for-granted by his family and his school that he would progress to university:

> And I don't think a lot of people at my school really did think about going straight into work, most people went to university, so it wasn't really something that people talked about that much, it was more about university and they prepared you a lot for it. It was a given that you would try and go to university.

These responses indicate the power of institutional and familial experiences to inculcate a middle-class orientation to HE that renders any other option unthinkable. The students did not, but more importantly, could not, think of doing anything but getting a degree.

Planning for an Imagined Future

So far, this chapter has discussed participants' orientation to university study and the people, processes and structures that shaped their journey into HE. We have explored the role of family and schooling in framing their horizons for action in relation to 'getting in' to their choice of university, establishing a difference between those who expected to go to university and those for whom it was seen as a hope rather than an entitlement. For many middle-class young people university is simply a taken-for-granted route, that they anticipate from an early age. For the young people on this route, going to university is seen as normal, perhaps even their right, both for the career opportunities a degree confers but also for the wider social and cultural benefits. Going to university becomes the default transition to adulthood, a contemporary rite of passage, indeed, for some, *not* going to university would be seen as unusual.

Nevertheless, whether going to university was taken-for-granted or a conscious decision out of step with family histories we discerned differences in students' approaches to their educational planning. Some students meticulously planned out their every move in relation to getting in to university with a clear view of a future career goal, while others had a more general view that they would like to progress to a graduate job, but did not have a specific career in mind. The final section of this chapter considers students' orientations to their imagined future (Ball et al. 2000) and how that was evident in what they told us in interviews.

For a number of young people, taking a degree was a long-term goal, and choices and actions were deliberately taken to achieve it. Determined planning was found amongst middle-class students who had a specific career ambition, but also amongst working-class students, where high academic achievement had opened up their horizons for action to consider a specific future career. This orientation was particularly visible amongst students such as Marcus (working-class UoB) and Craig (middle-class UoB) who selected an occupationally oriented subject (engineering). Marcus made a firm decision about his educational plans in his early teens, and then following them through all the way to university. He explained:

> Decided to get into engineering a long time ago, back in Year 9 started looking at possible careers. At that point I had a major interest in motor sport and ended up looking at some different universities for motor sport and went on some courses in the summer and sort of ended up choosing my GCSEs and A levels with an aim towards getting into some form of engineering. But then about 18 months ago went on a Physics lecture and it was given by people at Cambridge and some of the research started interesting me and sort of made me want to get into more generalized Engineering and ended up looking round at some more … well higher ranking institutes, and ended up looking at the likes of Cambridge and Imperial etcetera, but decided I didn't quite want the academic life that Cambridge tends to lead to in my opinion, didn't want to get stuck in research for the next 7 years, wanted a practical application of engineering. So I ended up choosing Bristol which, so far as I can see, is definitely the right decision for me. (Marcus, working-class, UoB)

Craig (middle-class, UoB) had also known what he wanted to do from a young age, but whereas Marcus slowly began to view higher-ranking institutions as a possibility, Craig started his choice process by using league tables to identify the top 20 institutions:

> I've kind of known since I was small I wanted to do engineering because my dad was an engineer and so there was always things being taken apart round our house. Whenever anything broke we never got a man in, it was always he'd fix it. So I always knew engineering was somewhere that I wanted to head to. And that worked as well with the subjects I liked and was good at, maths, physics, numbers things, logical things. So when it got to the time to look for a university, I started with just like one of those league table things of the top twentyish unis and thought "Where looks good? Where sounds like a decent place?" ordered a few prospectuses and read through them.

In contrast, for other participants education was not tied up with a specific career goal but it was nonetheless part of the overall plan for the direction of their lives. They were 'open planners', some with the tendency to drift along pathways that home and school backgrounds, as well as family expectations, had channelled them along. For many of the middle-class open planners it was a case of maximizing their potential by studying at the highest-ranking institution they could get into, sometimes regardless of subject. This was a way of keeping options open for delayed decision-making a point further down the line, whilst still strategically playing the game to maximize the value of their capitals.

Harriet, a middle-class student at UWE, was an example of how HE allowed middle-class students in particular to use HE as a passage to adulthood without a specific graduate career in mind, putting that part of the future on hold for three years (Ball et al. 2000):

> I did want to go to university; I didn't want to miss out on the whole experience of like growing up as well. Because my mum always said that, even if you're a bit unsure it is a good [way of] moving out for the first time, in a structured environment. I guess it's like a little stepping stone, you learn how to do everything together and look after yourself a bit more.

Sean (working-class, UoB) showed how strong the rhetoric is in the UK, that 'to get a good job you need a degree', and also how being successful academically at school makes HE a much more possible future:

> The job prospects are just far better if you go to university I think because of how many people go to university now especially. There would be an expectation that to get a good job you need a degree. But at the time I didn't really consciously think, I just thought I'd go to university because I was fairly bright. Yeah, and as most teenagers, I'd done some temporary work and jobs and didn't particularly find them very engaging or enjoyable.

He wanted to get a degree so he would have better job prospects, he wanted to 'become educated' and he wanted to learn more about politics, the subject he had chosen to study, but he also spoke of how he had not actively planned a future path for himself, but was looking to avoid temporary and uninspiring employment. HE as a choice was framed as both a positive choice related to an imagined future in a good job, and also as a way of escaping poor prospects associated with non-graduate employment.

Both determined planners and open planners had in view graduate labour market opportunities that were deemed more promising than any alternative routes. For some of the participants in our study, this involved getting back on track through the 'concerted intervention' of family, whereby parents mobilize their capital and their sense of how to play the game in order to intervene in the direction of young people's lives. In the final section, we discuss this process of what we call 'concerted intervention'.

Concerted Intervention: Getting Back on Track

Some students, although also positively choosing university, required help and intervention from family or school due to going off track at some point during their educational journey. This occurred where they lost interest in schooling or developed distracting interests or behaviours outside of school. However, despite losing motivation for education and further study, middle-class students had the luxury of being steered back on course by the intervention of others when they drifted too far from the educational path. Not only did parents make a concerted effort to steer their children back on track but also, in so doing, they cultivated an understanding of how to play the game to win. Our concept of concerted intervention is influenced by Lareau's (2002, 2003) notion of concerted cultivation, which is itself developed from Bourdieu's idea of cultural capital (discussed in Chapter 2). While concerted cultivation denotes the phenomenon of middle-class parents actively cultivating cultural capital in their children as a form of investment in their future resources, concerted intervention is more akin to the Bourdieusian notion of having 'a feel for the game'. Bourdieu describes this as follows:

> You can use the analogy of the game in order to say that a set of people take part in a rule-bound activity, an activity which, without necessarily being

the product of obedience to rules, obeys certain regularities. The game is the locus of an immanent necessity, which is at the same time an immanent logic. In the game you can't just do anything and get away with it. And the feel for the game, which contributes to this necessity and this logic, is a way of knowing this necessity and this logic. Whoever wants to win this game, appropriate the stakes, catch the ball... must have a feel for the game, that is, a feel for the necessity and the logic of the game. Should one talk of a rule? Yes and no. You can do so on condition that you distinguish clearly between rule and regularity. (Bourdieu 1990, p. 64)

We discerned a process of concerted intervention whereby parents, who while not articulating this as a set of rules, themselves have knowledge of the logic of the educational game and step in to play the game alongside their children in order to ensure that they do not drop the ball (to continue Bourdieu's metaphor).

Nicholas was an example of one such student who benefitted from concerted intervention to gain entry to university. His father was a professor of engineering, and Nicholas showed an early interest in the discipline, and a particular aptitude for maths. At an academically strong state school, Nicholas was identified as a 'gifted and talented' student. He wanted to go to Nottingham University, but failed to get the necessary grades, and was forced to resort to the UCAS clearing process; through which he gained a place at UWE. It was always assumed that he would do well at school and he told us that his parents and teachers always told him that he was clever. However, he failed to live up to his own and others' expectations:

N: They [my parents] made sure I revised and did my work, it wasn't a sign of pressure but there would always be the unspoken thing that they expected a lot out of me. Like my brother and my dad and my mum all did well academically and so on.

I: And what was their attitude when you went through Clearing and decided on UWE, what did they think?

N: I think my dad was slightly angry but my mum just told him to go for a walk whilst me, my brother and my mum sorted out Clearing. My mum was sympathetic ... yeah she was sympathetic towards it. Whereas my brother was just helping me, making sure I got through this Clearing process quickly, efficiently.

Nicholas not only provided an example of middle-class parents' assumption that their children will go to university, but also of the concerted intervention processes that come into play when the expected pathway becomes blocked. It became a family project to steer him and guide him back on track. In doing so his family's 'feel for the game' came into play and through 'efficiently' navigating the clearing system, they ensured that they left him in the best available position in the education field, at what they perceived to be the best university to which his grades would allow him to gain entry.

The efforts of working-class parents were less attuned to the logic of the game but were nonetheless motivated by a desire for their children to succeed educationally, which is exemplified by Arthur (working-class, UWE), whose story reveals how his mother intervened early on in his education:

> I was pretty badly behaved in Year 3 and 4, and then Year 4 I got put on report, and then that sorted me out basically ... just got into a bad group and also you thought it was cool to get in trouble. But then my mum found out, stopped some stuff and I buckled down.

Once back on track, Arthur's mother stepped back and allowed him to play the educational game in his own way, not demonstrating the same feel for the game as shown in the example with Nicholas above, and therefore not engaging in concerted intervention to ensure that the game worked in her son's favour. In Arthur's case, the intervention from his mother was to sort out an explicit problem and there was no notable steering through educational decision-making at later points. He was trusted to play the game alone. So his family did not seem to intervene in decisions about whether to go to university and what to study:

> I didn't think about university until half way through my GCSEs. At one point I was going to do a sporting qualification, probably full-time sport and I thought I'd do that until about six months before I did my decisions.

Another working-class student, Tracey, discussed her mother's strong desire for her to go to university, but there was no direct intervention to steer her down that route. She later reached the decision to do so after a year of working in a job she did not enjoy:

> my parents have always kind of tried to ... well my mum's always tried to push me to go to university, but I think that's because she obviously had me quite young and didn't get a chance to do that sort of thing. I came

out of sixth form not wanting to go to university any more, I'd just had enough of education, it was just driving me mad. And then I took a year out and got a 9 to 5 job and moved into a flat on my own. Absolutely hated it, so I just decided to go to university to get a job that I actually wanted.

However, having decided on a politics degree, she found the transition into university very challenging:

When I got here I expected that I might find it difficult, but then, because I was quite enthusiastic at first, I was really making an effort to keep up, and now I'm…just feeling a bit…I don't know, overwhelmed with it. And I just know it's going to get harder and harder and I can't even handle the first year of it. I think it's because I just changed what I wanted to do now, like my thoughts on what I want to do in the future have changed … it doesn't at all match up any more. I didn't expect this to happen though at all. I thought I had a plan, was going to negotiate the plan, and now it's all fallen apart.

Tracey's experience of university is discussed in more detail in the next chapter. She provides a good example of what can happen when working-class young people find themselves at university without it being a clear educational ambition. Despite support and encouragement to go to university from her mother, Tracey was not fully committed to gaining a degree. And while her mother hoped that she would continue Tracey played the game independently and decided to leave university. Like Arthur, above, parental intervention was less directive, and did not involve intervention in how to play the game.

CONCLUDING COMMENTS

This chapter has discussed how students' backgrounds influence their journey into university. Whilst we do not wish to be overly determin-istic, and acknowledge that there is room for agentic behaviour, our data *do* show how life choices are structured by social context. The school or college a young person attends has a significant impact on opportunities beyond the age of 18, but undoubtedly of greater con-sequence is the family background in which participants grew up. The students' narratives reveal how getting into university is not merely an individual project but a family endeavour. Reay (2000) has written about how giving their children the best educational opportunities they can is seen as the primary role for many middle-class mothers, more important than furthering their own careers. Our data demonstrates how, in many cases, this approach is continued beyond compulsory schooling and into HE. The expectations of family members, and the levels of capitals or resources upon which they are able to draw, play a significant role. Middle-class young people and their families can normally draw on an array of capitals to their advantage, while those from the working-classes tend to have to rely on personal resources and determination, backed up by emotional support from their families, rather than access to dominant cultural capital.

CHAPTER 5

Fitting In and Getting On

INTRODUCTION

This chapter focuses on how students make their way through under-graduate study once they have progressed to HE. We focus in particular on how students come to an understanding of their social class position-ing in relation to other students they encounter at university. We discuss processes of 'fitting in' in social and academic contexts, specifically casting light on narratives of students who have a sense of being 'a fish in water' or 'a fish out of water' as Bourdieu and Wacquant (1992, p. 127) define it:

> When habitus encounters a social world of which it is the product, it is like a "fish in water": it does not feel the weight of the water, and it takes the world about itself for granted.

We highlight a phenomenon that has only been implicit in previous literature—middle-class students who feel themselves to be 'a fish out of water' at a modern university. We discuss how their responses to being a fish out of water are quite different from those of working-class students at the elite university in our study, who can also have a sense of not quite fit-ting in. We explore how students engage in building up capitals—and the ways in which middle-class students at both universities successfully engage in the concerted cultivation of capitals, through CV building. The chap-ter first of all considers the working-classes and middle-classes within the overall context of each institution, providing details of the class make-up

A.M. Bathmaker et al., *Higher Education, Social Class and Social Mobility*, DOI 10.1057/978-1-137-53481-1_5

73

of each institution and the students' sense of fit within the environment. The chapter then discusses the ways in which students are positioned to draw upon, and develop, forms of capital, particularly highlighting *the hypermobilization* of capital of the middle-class students at UWE.

WORKING-CLASS STUDENTS AT THE UNIVERSITY OF BRISTOL

Fitting In

Working-class students are in a minority at the University of Bristol, and when they are found they tend to be from the upper working-classes (few students in our study had parents from NS-SEC category 7). According to HESA, in 2010 (the year the students entered HE), only 14 % of the undergraduate intake of University of Bristol students were from NS-SEC categories 4–7, which broadly correlates with working-class backgrounds, as discussed in Chapter 2. The national average in England for this particular year's intake of students from these categories is 31 %. Not only are these students in a minority at the University of Bristol, but they are under-represented at the university when compared with the national picture of working-class university attendance.

We were interested in understanding how it feels to be a student for three years at an institution where much of the population is highly privileged. Much has been made of the sense of 'not belonging' for working-class students confronted with elite university experience (Reay 1998; Reay et al. 2009, 2010; Crozier and Reay 2011), and we wished to explore how, and if, these feelings remain or shift over the student life course. Initially, we discerned some familiar patterns of experience, supporting the findings of previous studies. When confronted with the extreme privilege of the University of Bristol and its high proportion of privately educated and wealthy students, many of our working-class students indeed felt themselves to be 'fish out of water'. The reasons for these feelings were difficult for the students to pin down; it was more of a sense of not being quite the 'right' sort of person, or of being a 'body out of place' (Puwar 2004; The Res-Sisters 2016). As one participant, Samantha, put it, 'it's like unwritten rules', which appear to operate as constraints on behaviour and social mixing:

> When we went on the field trip at the very beginning of the year to get to know each other, I was one of the few people from a state school, and

that straight away separated me from...or I felt it separated me... from the [fee-paying] public school, or the private school people. And it shouldn't do, it shouldn't make a difference, but for some reason it does, and it just makes it more difficult, like if I suddenly start talking to them, I'd find it weird and they'd find it weird. I don't know why, they say there isn't a class barrier, but there is, and I notice it quite a lot. (Samantha, working-class, UoB)

The important thing here is that Samantha feels and notices the difference. The 'difference' was hers to recognize as the outsider to the majority group. None of the middle-class students at the University of Bristol recognized class or indeed 'race' as an issue, precisely because their privileged positions allowed them to be blinkered to the world beyond their bubble (see Chapter 7 for more on this in relation to 'race'). But for working-class students, the divisions of class were acutely felt:

Samantha: I feel the division of people, and I shouldn't, but I do. But it just makes life a bit more difficult.

Interviewer: You say you feel the division.

Samantha: Mmm, like codes of social conduct sort of thing. Like I just wouldn't speak to certain people, and certain people just wouldn't speak to me. It's kind of like at school when you have the 'populars' and the 'geeks' and they don't converse; they are two separate groups. It's kind of like the same thing. I think that's how it feels sometimes.

These 'codes of conduct' are regulated by interactions with middle-class peers, who convey their sense of superiority or disapproval through their exclusive words and actions. In our first interviews with students, we learned that on arrival at the University of Bristol, new students' conversations would fixate on previous schooling experience. Perhaps this is unsurprising, given that schooling was most likely to be their immediate prior experience. However, coded in this discussion is an assumption that students will recognize and be able to place each other according to their school background, perhaps finding common ground or common friends and acquaintances. This points to an upper middle-class and privately educated milieu, where the private school matrix develops social connections through shared cultural experiences such as inter-school matches, debating societies, and even socializing (particularly for those who attended public schools in London) which can then be utilized and strengthened at Oxford, Cambridge, and the Russell Group universities. For students from state schools, this topic of conversation is a non-starter because it is highly unlikely to expose points of connection or common ground. Therefore, the very fact that school attended is a significant topic excludes and marginalizes those on the outside of the private school system. Zoe powerfully illustrated this exclusion:

> I think that [University] Hall is very pretentious, a lot of people there walk around with family crests, the Lords and Ladies. You know [TV star], his son is there actually in my Hall. I had dinner with him last night … well I didn't actually have dinner with him, I was sat on the bench while he was there. It's all that sort of borderline aristocracy there, everybody goes "oh I went to Thailand" and, you know, that sort of thing. The first question they ask you is "what school did you go to?" and I was like "[XX] Comp", it's that sort of atmosphere. (Zoe, working-class, UoB)

Zoe's reaction to finding herself ill at ease and out of place was to take a critical and derisive view of privilege. As an outsider, she had to negotiate her position and, through recognition of her own resources of independence, she found value in her non-privileged position. She was aware that she had had to work hard to get to where she was and she drew upon this to sustain her throughout the degree. The following extract is just one of many examples where Zoe demonstrated her resilience:

> Zoe: I don't feel intimidated because it's laughable, people who judge based on whatever money you have or whatever status, because at the end of the day they've not earned that for themselves, that's just been given to them on a plate. And the way I look at it is they're all privileged but I'm going to work for myself and whatever I do, I just want to be successful in it so that I can turn around and be like "ha, I've got everything that I want in the world and I didn't have to take it from anyone else, I acquired it myself". And that is so much more valuable than just being given it.

Similarly, Samantha found herself swimming against the current and needing to take a defiant stance in order to survive. On a field trip she was made to feel like an outsider because she went to a state school, unlike most of the other young women in the dormitory she was sharing:

> And then we were talking in the room about schools and what A-levels we'd done and there was me and one other girl from a state school, and she

[one of the privately educated young women] was like "really, you went to a state school?" And I was like "there's nothing wrong with my state school thank you very much, it's fine, it got me As and it got me the grades that I needed to get here the same as your private school did, just you paid for it". (Samantha, working-class, UoB)

These examples are illustrative of the ways in which the working-classes are cast as outsiders within an elite higher education environment, yet they provide glimpses of how they can, and do, navigate their way through the uncharted waters. Bourdieu describes an '*implicit collusion* among all the agents who are the products of similar conditions and conditionings' (Bourdieu 2000, p. 145) which operates to define quietly ways of being and not being in different spaces. Working-class students did not share the same past conditions and conditionings as their privileged peers and so they did not have the luxury of operating in the same taken-for-granted way. Instead, they were prompted to be reflexive about their interactions, their tastes and their judgements and, in doing so, had to draw upon personal resources to overcome the negative positioning that others imposed on them.

Getting On

It is often rather uncritically assumed that working-class students who have attended state schools will experience difficulties fitting in to an academic milieu which is at odds with their class milieu, and that, consequently, they will need 'special help' with study skills, such as note taking, essay planning and writing, and different techniques of reading. This is a 'deficit' reading of working-class cultural capital, though aspects of HE practices such as the use of language and literary references by tutors may fall outside the stocks of cultural capital possessed by working-class young people. However, a key finding of our study was that students from *all* class backgrounds found the transition from school to university learning regimes very difficult. This related to the switch from what students regularly described as spoon-feeding to independent study and private research. As Liam (middle-class, UoB) put it:

You know they expect you to do a lot of work outside of lectures, which obviously is a culture shock for everyone, like all the extra reading and stuff.

The problem of spoon-feeding was actually more acute for students from private schools since they had received far more individual support from teachers adept at getting people through exams. Liam, for example, repeatedly compared his university experience negatively in comparison to school:

> I think obviously as well, coming from a private school with sort of fees of like nine grand, you know, at school I was used to the very best sort of standard of teaching, and you've just got to realise that at university (a) you're expected to do a lot more on your own, and (b) university is for everyone, not just the people who can afford to pay for the best, which I can no longer do but I could just about do through school. It was quite hard, and they basically just sort of left you to sink or swim. Whereas at school, you know, I didn't actually need it at school, that's probably going to sound arrogant, but then you know, they obviously gave you a lot of help and obviously a lot more contact hours and stuff. So yeah it was a change, it was obviously more independent, more academically focused ... it was just a lot more independent study, slightly different sort of focus from basically gearing you towards your exams like they do in school.

The working-class students, as shown in the last chapter, had less support from both school and parents, and so were more used to taking the initiative for themselves. The adjustment process for them was as much, if not *more*, social rather than intellectual.

The challenge of navigating the middle-class milieu as a working-class student engendered critiques of and reflections on class practices. Drawing on their encounters with peers, they observed that private schools produced spoon-fed young people who were not capable enough to continue to achieve highly once they had to think independently. Garry typified these observations.

> Let's use [male flatmate] as an example. His parents have invested a lot, a lot of money in his education. He's been privately educated all throughout secondary school and sixth form. But now he's out of that sort of being spoon-fed information by that private school environment, he's struggling, to tell you the truth. He got 60 last year, just, but he's probably going to get a 2:2 this year. (Garry, working-class, UoB)

Beyond the idea that private schools enable parents with money to ensure educational achievement regardless of their child's ability, Garry formulated a criticism of the parenting practices of the privileged. In his analysis, the middle-class child is constructed as a commodity to be financially invested in, in order to realize a good return:

> [H]is dad's a barrister, very busy, and his mum's an educational psychologist, again very busy. I have no idea what sort of hours they worked when he was growing up or anything but it just seems to be a perception that they invested a lot of money but not maybe necessarily time. And like whenever they come to visit him he always gets really paranoid and is like 'I've got to make sure my notes are in order, they might want to check my notes'... It's almost like they see his education as their investment and they want to check on their investment to see how the money they have put into it, how that's working out for them. I don't know, it just seems like they've tried to replace time with money.

Garry compared this experience with his own, where his single mother worked but also spent a lot of time on him. In this way, he challenged the middle-class milieu in which he found himself and privileged his own classed family experiences. As part of the experience of attending an elite institution, the working-class students are required to negotiate their classed cultural identities and positions in relation to the middle-class norm. The result is a complex mix of conforming to middle-class cultural norms and resisting them with critical reflection. This was further exemplified in the following reflections of Marcus, who could see value in his less privileged upbringing whilst problematizing the value of what was produced by upper middle-class experiences:

> Considering my background and getting to university ... I've not come from a private school, which so many of my friends have, and actually the one thing I've always had from that I felt was maybe a bit more of an understanding, or tolerance and idea of the real world. (Marcus, working-class, UoB)

So he explained that:

> Living in my house, I'm the one who is in charge of the house, and there's a distinct lack of common sense amongst my southern friends. [...] I mean some of them ... some of their actions, you do at times maybe wonder how on earth they've managed to dress themselves in the mornings!

In navigating their way through a world that is not their own (Bourdieu and Eagleton 1992; Ingram and Abrahams 2016) some working-class students were forced to confront their own and others' taken-for-granted ways of being and to reflect on the value of cultural practices. In this case, Marcus asserted the value of his own working-class cultural capital, or 'experiential capital' (Bradley and Ingram 2012). The navigation between two worlds gave the working-class students a double vantage point, which promoted reflexivity and a way of being multi-faceted. This is summed up nicely in the following statement from Garry:

> Just things…in terms of tastes and friendship groups. In the first year I'd avoid mixing the two—well not deliberately avoid but just happen to sort of associate with my work and home friends away from uni, and the uni friends away from them because, I don't know, conversations are very different, they wouldn't be very compatible. So you learn to have a certain side of yourself that you present to a certain group of people, and certain discourses that you wouldn't have with others. So you learn to be, I don't know, what's the word? Multi-faced.

For the working-class students at an elite institution there were cultural negotiations taking place throughout their undergraduate experience (see Abrahams and Ingram 2013). It is worth noting again that what we are defining as cultural struggle does not assume cultural lack or deficit. However, we did discern certain disadvantages in terms of forms of capital and discuss this in the following section.

Differential Forms of Capital

Many working-class students could not access the same resources as their middle-class counterparts and this impacted on their capacity to utilize university as the vehicle for social mobility, which it is often simplistically expected to be. Unsurprisingly we found that working-class students experienced more financial constraints and this impacted on the sorts of activities they could participate in outside of their formal studies. These activities included both extra-curricular activities (ECA) and employment-related activities, such as work experience and internships (Bathmaker et al. 2013).

There were two distinct constraints on working-class students' chances of engaging in ECA, and these could both be attributed to economic capital. First of all, participation in many ECAs were expensive, even seemingly low-cost sports such as football and rugby were prohibitive because of kit costs and club fees. Worse still, were less everyday sports, such as snow sports as Alfie (working-class, UWE) explained:

> The only problem with quite a lot of them is that they're quite expensive to go into and I can't afford really to go into them. Snow sports looks quite good but you have to pay to go to the dry slope every weekend. They have about five holidays or something and they're like £500 each so it's a bit too much ... I think gliding is about £80 a lesson, which is good compared to normal, you know going to an actual airfield, but it's still a bit too much. I think a lot of it's sort of aimed at richer students really.

The second economic constraint on working-class students' engagement with ECA was that they were more likely than their middle-class counterparts to have to work during term time in order to survive. This had a knock-on effect on their chances of committing to ECA involvement. ECAs comprise part of a rounded CV and constraints on participation could be seen as a potential disadvantage in terms of future employment.

A more explicit disadvantage faced by working-class students was in terms of social capital acquisition and mobilization. Their families simply did not have the connections to draw upon to offer advantages in the competitive world of student internships or accessing top professions. The examples below were typical responses:

> I find it so weird when people have parents that are lawyers or doctors and they can get you work experience in a hospital or...I just think "that's crazy" that's like something I've never experienced. Because my parents do just ordinary jobs. I don't know how they would help me. I don't think they would be able to. (Anna, working-class, UoB)

> It's not that they won't give me help, my parents are the most helpful people I could ever imagine. It's just I don't know whether they've got the skills to be able to find me what I want, because I know what I'm looking for, it's not really a "them" sort of thing. (Zoe, working-class, UoB)

These students described their parents as incredibly supportive. The disadvantages they faced were that their social capital did not match up to their aspirations as students who sought careers outside of the field occupied by their families.

WORKING-CLASS STUDENTS AT UWE

Fitting In

Compared with the University of Bristol, the University of the West of England is a more socially diverse institution. Statistics from HESA show that 29 % of 2010 entrants to UWE were from NS-SEC 4–7, compared with 14 % at UoB (against a national average of 31 %). This could potentially make the working-class students more at ease with themselves and their class position. They are less likely to be fish out of water, as there are a significant number of other people who occupy similar class positions. One of the working-class participants, Kyle, put it like this:

> Class doesn't [matter] here I wouldn't say because you've got such an array and it's hard to sort of quantify, classify people, and people aren't really that bothered in doing so.

His comment echoes previous research, which has shown that working-class students often feel a better sense of fit with a modern or post-92 institution rather than an elite one (Reay 2001; Reay et al. 2009). Roberts (2010, p. 221) notes that the rise in participation by young people from working-class families has been at lower-ranked institutions and suggests that: 'at all levels in the social class structure, students appear to self-select towards universities that are perceived to be "for people like me"'. Moreover, evidence that working-class students are found predominantly in lower-ranked institutions, while students from established middle-class and upper middle-class families dominate in the highest-ranked universities indicates how this sense of fit reflects stratification in the HE field not just by 'type' of institution, but by socio-economic background of students attending those institutions (Boliver 2013). We largely found evidence to support a 'working-class fit' with UWE, the post-92 institution in our study, a connection that seemed to form even before entry. Isabel, for example, talked about her ease and sense of comfort with the institution, despite encouragement from her teacher to apply to the more prestigious University of Bristol:

> [UWE] would have been my first choice even though I know my law teacher told me that Bristol University would probably look better on your application to a solicitors' firm. Yeah, I didn't apply anyway, I just ...**I felt**

comfortable here and I think that's quite important, I didn't want to have to feel nervous when I go to university or feel like I'm really ... I don't know, there's a sort of vibe about Bristol I get, like it would be more competitive and not as relaxed, so I didn't really want to have that worry and I thought I'd just come here. Not "just come here" but "I do want to come here". (Isabel, working-class, UWE)

Although our findings generally support a match between working-class students and the University of the West of England, we do not wish to suggest that this was straightforwardly so for all of the working-class cohort. At times, the students indeed felt themselves to be fish out of water. The seminar room in particular was a place where working-class students felt exposed or under threat. Tracey, whose story was discussed in the previous chapter, recounted her discomfort and humiliation at being marked out as different because of her perspective on issues within her politics class. The following story was framed by a discussion of being humiliated by a privileged young man in her class, who she explained was 'really different' from her, and who derided her for the lack of sophistication in her thinking:

A lot of the time I think I'd get on with people who were different to me, but there were a few people on the course that I really felt were just constantly attacking things that I said ...like it was quite humiliating sometimes when I said something and they'd just be like "oh no". (Tracey, working-class, UWE)

Tracey struggled with these sorts of encounters and with feeling at ease and happy with university and eventually dropped out altogether after her first year. She was an example of a working-class 'fish out of water' at UWE for whom the weight of the water was too much. Tracey's way of dealing with being out of place contrasted greatly with the middle-class 'fish out of water' in her institution, discussed later in this chapter. Like Zoe and Samantha from UoB, Tracey drew upon her own determination and strength to navigate her way through university, but her resolve was eventually undermined. Rather than her own personal failing, she was arguably a casualty of a system that has a long way to go to provide a space for the working-classes to feel culturally valued. It is important to stress that in highlighting working-class struggles, we are not presenting our students as culturally lacking. Rather, we are suggesting that the middle-class field of HE lacks cultural sensitivity to those other than the white middle-classes (see Chapter 7 for a discussion of 'race' and ethnicity).

Getting On

The lack we did perceive with regards to the working-classes was in terms of economic capital. Not only were working-class students more likely to have to take up paid employment to survive at university, but they also were more likely to worry about their finances. This response from Adele was typical:

> I get very stressed about my financial situation, and sometimes I think about that more than I do about my uni studies. So I'm worried about that in the second and third year when your studies really do count towards your degree, because you get so stressed about where your rent's going to come from and how you're going to buy food and stuff, that it completely over-shadows anything else that you're doing. (Adele, working-class, UWE)

Isabel's comments provided further evidence of working-class financial struggles:

> I bought a laptop with my student loan because mine packed up, so I've just been like really behind on money. I don't ask my parents for money or anything ... we were just in a lecture and she was talking about employment contracts, and she said "who of you here gets paid work" and only about three people put their hands up, I couldn't believe it. A lot of people just rely on their loans or their parents. That was shocking really. (Isabel, working-class, UWE)

What is highlighted here is not just that Isabel had to work but that she valued the financial independence from her parents. On her law course few other people claimed to be involved in paid employment. Her comments about other students' reliance on parents and student finance was supported by our data with evidence that many privileged students had their accommodation costs paid for by parents, received monthly parental allowances on top of student loans, and had trust funds to pay for their education. Some students reported parents sending online supermarket deliveries, and others reported that they took out student loans, even if not needed, and invested in bonds, as they were seen as the cheapest form of debt they could ever have.

MIDDLE-CLASS STUDENTS AT BRISTOL

Fitting In

At the University of Bristol, the middle-class students (those whose parents occupy the professional job categories designated as NS-SEC 1–3) make up most of the population. In the 2010 intake, 86 % of students were from this privileged background. Additionally, a critical mass of students came from privately educated backgrounds. HESA data for the 2010/2011 cohort shows that only 60.2 % of the UoB population was from state educated backgrounds. This helps to ensure that the privileged classes find themselves at home within the institution. Indeed, just as the working-class students may have a sense of fitting in better at the University of the West of England before entry, the middle-classes often knew that the University of Bristol was a place that worked for them before they even set foot on the precinct. Elliot, for example, described not even needing to visit the university but knowing just what he could expect:

> No I didn't go to any Open Days. It's purely on reputation. I came to Bristol once before but I kind of ... know what to expect from universities. Well I think I've been confirmed in that view because **it's exactly how I expected**. (Elliot, middle-class, UoB)

Elliot demonstrated an expectation to go university and more importantly a confident understanding of what he was going to find there. In saying that Bristol lived up to his expectations in terms of what a university would be like, he exposed his understanding as based on the idea of a traditional, old university. Elliot was educated in a very elite public school and in later interviews stated that his seamless transition to university was aided by the fact that he found himself surrounded by many former pupils from his school. Sometimes, he showed an awareness of his own privilege and was reflective about it. However, this is not the case with all of the privileged students. Often privilege was very much taken-for-granted, even denied.

Liam, for example, described himself as the 'perfect public school boy' yet presented his family position and his educational achievement as one of sacrifice. He emphasized both the financial outlay and personal sacrifice involved in ensuring he got to 'one of the best universities in the country':

> So any sort of stereotypes of an overly privileged private school sort of stereotype I don't think really applies because I have had to make sacrifices as to where I've been able to get to university [by sacrifice he means giving up a chance to play Rugby at Twickenham as the training was taking up too much study time], because it's not beating around the bush because Bristol is one of the best universities in the country. Everyone knows that obviously Oxbridge is the pinnacle but underneath that you've got a layer of the Bristols, the Durhams, the 3 London universities, and maybe somewhere like Warwick as well. So I had to make a lot of sacrifices for that, to be here, so did my mum and dad, to the tune of nigh on £100,000 and a lot of time and effort. (Liam, middle-class, UoB)

His comments also highlight a middle-class understanding of the university system. The assumption about which universities are 'best' is based on reputation and tradition, and what 'everyone knows'. Best becomes defined by highest valued symbolic commodity and judgement does not entail consideration of qualities beyond which degree certificate carries most weight. The middle-classes can expect to be in the upper echelons of the university hierarchy but importantly they, like Liam, can view these spaces as ones they are entitled to occupy because of their efforts and achievements. The view they cultivate disregards the notion of their own educational privilege.

Getting On

In contrast to the examples above, we found that whether they were aware of it or not middle-class students at UoB were very well positioned to exploit their existing forms of capital. For some highly strategic middle-class students, being competitive could be read as their taken-for-granted dispositions towards university and career advancement. Nathan was one example, whose interviews from the outset showed clear career strategizing, as well as a world view where competition was inevitable, desirable and also cut-throat, as demonstrated in the following comment:

> Everyone has As at GCSEs, you've just got to try and differentiate yourself by doing something extra like Investment Society, or an internship,

or do mooting. Because you see some of these people—particularly if you want to become a barrister—it's ridiculous, you see these people who, you know, run a soup kitchen in their spare time, got a first class honours in their degree, been to Africa and saved a school from famine, you know, it's absolutely ridiculous how much they have. So you've got to try and aim for that or try to match it, try and build up your CV because it's so competitive. (Nathan, middle-class, UoB)

While some students strategically mobilized available capital to secure internships, others simply took such advantages for granted. David (middle-class, UoB) talked about his work experience without mentioning the role his family connections played in the process. However, when probed he revealed the extent of the help received:

Well I guess this interview I had over Easter was through a family friend who is the partner of the firm so hopefully that would help. Saying that, my previous work experience last summer was through one of my dad's contacts, so I guess there's always the chance [of finding] something through them.

Elliot, a middle-class student at UoB who wanted to work in journalism, was casual about the help his parents could provide:

Well my dad worked for the BBC, he does a job every year. He runs a conference, oh no, streams a conference, so he might get me a job there this time in the kind of PR, just doing press releases all the time, which would be tedious and quite hard work, but it's only for a week and it's in Abu Dhabi.

These students' lack of recognition of their privileged position appeared to stem from a taken-for-granted disposition towards opportunity, considering such opportunity their entitlement.

MIDDLE-CLASS STUDENTS AT UWE

Fitting In

Whereas 86 % of new undergraduates at the University of Bristol were from middle-class backgrounds in 2010, well over the national average of 69 %, at the University of the West of England, a considerably smaller percentage, 71 % of students, were from NS-SEC 1–3 families. This figure is higher than the English national average of 69 % for the 2010 intake year, and it is high for a post-92 institution. However, the middle-classes who take up places at UWE are less likely than at Bristol to be from the more privileged end of the middle-class spectrum, and a much smaller proportion of the UWE population are from privately educated backgrounds. 2010/2011 HESA figures indicate that 91 % of entrants at UWE were state educated compared with 60.2 % at UoB.

Despite having a relatively high percentage of working-class students the middle-classes comprise the majority population, and many of the middle-class participants felt comfortable at UWE, as we found with working-class students. Some of the middle-class students named particular reasons for attending a post-1992 university. Natasha, for example, explained that she was attracted by the idea of having a lot of academic support from lecturers:

> I think that's why I chose UWE as well because you can just e-mail someone and ask a question, you know. [Elsewhere] they're researchers rather than teachers, and I think at the open day, the course leader made it really clear that at UWE it's basically not as much of a step up because they're more like teachers than…you know, you e-mail someone and they get back to you in half an hour. They're really helpful. (Natasha, middle-class, UWE)

For others, being at UWE provided them with an opportunity to stand out academically. Donna, for example, was from a family on an upward trajectory. She was using the high economic and social capital of her father to maintain her pathway, adding to this by increasing her levels of cultural capital through successful participation in HE. She came from the outskirts of London. Her father worked as an IT consultant at an investment bank in the city and had attended university, but as a mature student, rather than straight from school. Her mother had also completed HE study to train as a teacher, though she became what Donna described as a 'stay-at-home' mother when the children were born. Donna was studying economics at UWE and appeared to feel at home, framing her decision to study there as a positive choice. She justified choosing UWE over Loughborough when applying to university as follows:

> UWE's a polytechnic [sic], it's sort of more applied to real life, whereas I think at Loughborough it was much more academic.

But her choice also fitted in with a strategy of making the most of her resources and capabilities. UWE required BBB grades for admission rather than AAB at Loughborough, and it became clear over subsequent interviews, that she judged UWE to be a place where she could stand out. She was determined from early on to achieve a first class degree, and described her strategies for ensuring this:

> I'm trying to aim to get firsts, like I really don't like missing my lectures and stuff. Because apart from one module all of them are exam based, or like mostly exam based, so if I miss a lecture I can't catch up. A lot of my friends…they only have eight hours a week but because their course is so coursework based they just catch up like that. But if I continuously miss something, the notes on Blackboard are good but they're not as good as someone teaching it to you. (Donna, middle-class, UWE)

With some notable exceptions, discussed in the final section of this chapter, the middle-class students in our sample framed their choice to study at UWE in positive terms, as a choice which reflected their educational achievements and family expectations. There were plenty of examples of middle-class 'fish-in-water'. Two students, however, stood out in this respect, and viewed the university as 'not the place for a person like me'. For Francesca and Oscar, UWE was *not* the destination of choice. Both of these students were from highly educated families with high cultural capital. The final section of this chapter draws upon the cases of these two students, as this phenomenon of middle-class fish out of water has received little attention in previous research. Before we turn to this, we consider more generally how middle-class students 'get on' at UWE.

Middle-class students in both institutions were more successful than their working-class counterparts in gaining access to internships, particularly in high-status areas such as law or banking, even though many working-class students had clear internship goals and were achieving top grades on their courses. Largely, this was down to middle-class social capital advantage. While working-class students were unlikely to have contacts in big companies to help them, middle-class students could frequently draw on significant connections to secure the best internships. It was striking how the social capital most often employed was firmly embedded in family networks, as the following examples show:

It's a case of who you know not what you know in some cases. So I am try-ing to pull in any family ties … like my dad's quite friendly with one of the traders at [Bank]. He was head of the internship scheme … and my mum's a governor at my old school and one of the governors was a trader at [Bank], so I am trying to pull some strings there too. (Dylan, middle-class, UWE)

My dad's quite high up in engineering, so like advises the government, so a lot of people owe him a lot of favours around the country. If everything doesn't go well this summer, I can pretty much go to France and study in Lyon for a couple of months, because people owe him a lot of favours there. (Nicholas, middle-class, UWE)

In both cases, these students had an awareness of the capital they pos-sessed and were predisposed to utilizing this fully. They knew how to "pull strings" and capitalize on "favours" owed to family members.

Middle-Class Fish Out of Water and the 'Hyper-Mobilization' of Capital
As with some of the middle-class UoB students discussed above, the UWE middle-class 'fish out of water' identified strongly with high-status HE institutions. It could be described as part of the familial habitus (Reay 1998) in that these students had internalized a perception of what con-stitutes a 'good' university education. Both students had a long ranging and deep family connection with traditional universities (each had a parent educated to doctoral level and each had family members who were univer-sity lecturers in elite institutions), which helped to frame what was think-able, acceptable, and expected in terms of educational pathways. A post-92 institution did not fall within their 'horizons for action' (Hodkinson and Sparkes 1997, p. 34) and so, when forced to conceive of themselves as post-92 students, Francesca and Oscar both struggled to make the iden-tity leap. Oscar summed this up in the following excerpt, which is from his first interview, where he immediately confessed all his difficulties with being at an institution where he did not feel he belonged:

I'm a UWE student who feels like they should be at Bristol, if you want to put it that way. I come from a very strong university background. My mother's father, my grandfather, was a lecturer at Cambridge. My aunt was a lecturer at Harvard but now she's a lecturer at Warwick. And since before I was … you know, since when I was very, very young I learnt to look down on an ex poly before I even knew what it was, you know, "oh you don't want to go to an ex poly". You hear about the universities that are worth …

and I've expressed these views back to the people I hear this kind of stuff from and they were kind of, you know, shocked "oh ..." They're not snobs, they're not bad people but it's just one of those things. The universities you hear talked about in conversation are Durham, York, Warwick, you know, Cambridge, Oxford, Edinburgh, UCL, those universities. (Oscar, middle-class, UWE)

Within Oscar's world, the polytechnic-university divide survives despite the fact that institutions have not existed as 'polytechnics' within his life-time. The language is resurrected through family discourse as a form of boundary drawing in which the middle-classes distance themselves from the masses in order to maintain advantage through reputational status and positioning of institutions in the face of higher education expansion.

Similarly, for Francesca, UWE was not the university of choice but was outside her comfort zone. Initially she had considered more presti-gious universities (Sussex, Kent, the University of East Anglia, Exeter and Sheffield), based on 'reputation and what I thought of it on the day when I went and when I spoke to people.' However, her A level results were a great disappointment to her. She achieved BBC instead of her predicted results of A*BB, and was not accepted at her chosen universities. She went into the clearing system (a centralized system whereby universities with places left are matched with students who have not been offered places at their chosen institutions) and UWE was the first place she was offered. Although her family was supportive, and her father looked at the UWE website and assured her 'that a lot of the teachers here had done a lot of research in their own sort of specialisms', UWE was completely outside her world. This was a further example of the concerted intervention of middle-class parents discussed in Chapter 4. Francesca explained:

No-one I know from my school came here [UWE] apart from one other. No-one from my sixth form came here apart from one other guy who also came through 'clearing' to do the same course. So I only know him, nobody else when I came here. So the other places—a couple of people went to Falmouth, a couple of people went to Sheffield. [...] A lot of my friends went to Bristol University.

Where Reay et al. (2009) discuss the 'shock of the elite' for working-class students when they are confronted with the strange world of the elite uni-versity, in our study we discerned a 'shock *for* the elite' when the middle-classes with high cultural capital were confronted with the unfamiliar world of a middle-ranking institution. Just as Reay et al.'s working-class students were prompted to a state of reflexive awareness of themselves and their surroundings through the strangeness of their new world so too did our students come face to face with an image of themselves rendered anew against an unfamiliar backdrop. Their reflexive awareness was heightened through confronting themselves in a place they were not meant to exist. Often, this was a discomfiting experience, as it forced deep-seated conceptions to the surface to be considered and challenged:

> The people on my course, I probably wouldn't have socialized…well not necessarily socialized, just talked to, not actively avoiding them, just not being in the situation. Because…I don't know, it's probably not great to class people, or like stereotype people, but…I don't know, I really don't know how to explain it without sounding really bad. (Francesca)

It was difficult for Francesca to admit to not wanting to be around people who were not from a similar background to her and she described herself as 'very, very different'. She had been thrown out of her comfort zone into a place that was at odds with her sense of identity. She said:

> In my first year, I felt very … not an outcast because I still felt like it was fine, but I felt like there weren't many people like me I guess, and there was a lot of people that were similar to each other and I wasn't really part of the identity I guess of UWE.

Typically, middle-class young people negotiate educational spaces as fish in water. Their habitus aligns with the institution and their ways of thinking are in accordance with institutional expectations. As a fish out of water, Francesca could no longer take the world about her for granted. It was new, hostile, and misaligned with her sense of self. Oscar experienced the same sense of not belonging, again with the surfacing of uncomfortable hither-to taken-for-granted assumptions about the social world:

> I'd hope to find other people like me who have kind of fallen from … I'm such a snob. You know, just fallen from a perhaps higher academic level. There's no way of talking about it without sounding pretty awful. I should also state I am massively against the private school system—massively, but

inevitably I have a lot of friends who went there, you know, just because of the kind of people I get on with. And so all that kind of elitist infrastructure that exists in the education system I disapprove of. So it's not like I want to be part of some kind of fraternity of absolutely top level university, that's not the kind of thing that I seek. I think one of my biggest worries about coming here was my contemporaries, which is so unfair, totally unfair, it's based on no fact, but that was inevitably a worry of mine.

Oscar here demonstrated that he was grappling with feelings that he recognized were worthy of critique. He knew they were 'awful' things to think and tried to justify them through expressions of liberal views on the education system. There was a contradiction between his critical views on the elitist UK education system and his desire to be educated amongst the educationally privileged. In subsequent discussions, he bemoaned the fact that few of his university peers were from families where both parents have university degrees, a reluctant demonstration of reputational affect, whereby UWE students are deemed intellectually inferior to students positioned in universities of higher rank and reputation.

Getting On

Both the middle-class fish out of water at UWE and the working-class fish out of water at UoB had to cope with the unnerving feelings of not belonging but did so in different ways. As discussed earlier, working-class students had to muster reserves of strength and resilience to navigate their way through an alien and somewhat hostile environment. While on the one hand it could be argued that the middle-class fish out of water at UWE had to draw up similar levels of strength to deal with an alien world, on the other hand, they were buffered by layers of capital which they could utilize to maximize their position and ease their anxieties.

Both Francesca and Oscar recognized that, although important, the degree certificate was only one part of the overall package that they needed to create in order to further their careers. Francesca had already completed placements every year for three years before starting university, at a Barristers' Chambers in London, at an international law firm in the City of London, and at another international law firm. She had mobilized her social capital to gain access to experience with prestigious organizations, using her father's social contacts, her friend's father who was head of a Chambers in London, and capitalizing on having a neighbour who worked in another Chambers. Despite feeling as if she was in the wrong place Francesca was able to draw on a range of resources, including considerable family economic capital, in order to seize unpaid internship opportunities offered as part of her degree course:

> I'm working for six weeks [...] and I'm paying them [...]. I'm not allowed to be paid, the uni isn't allowing me to be paid, and their company don't pay interns anyway. [...] I have to pay for the flights, I have to pay for my accommodation, I have to pay for food. I pay for the privilege of working for the company, and pay the insurance, visa, everything. [...] My parents will fund it all [...] because I wouldn't be able to pay that much because I don't work.

This hypermobilization of capitals was also in evidence in Francesca's extensive knowledge of what was necessary to become a successful barrister, the career to which she aspired. She explained in detail the need to join the right clubs and associations and participate in lunches and events where she would meet judges, in anticipation of training for the Bar, and was preparing herself to do this. UWE, like UoB, offers opportunities to do these things. She continued with sports and hobbies she had developed an interest in before university and saw them as both a social outlet and a form of CV building, ensuring that she was not just a member of a society, but taking up a committee role in the sports society she had joined.

Oscar's approach was less purposeful, in that he did not have a specific career in mind to work towards. Despite this, he said he felt the need to use his university time productively in order to develop his interests and skills beyond his course. This seemed to link to a sense of guilt he attached to wasting time. Like Francesca, he had significant interests in sports and music that he had developed from the concerted cultivation that took place during his childhood (Lareau 2002, 2003).

> Oscar: Well, I played the trumpet a lot when I was younger and like [my college] were saying the big band, wind band orchestra all that kind of stuff ... having taken two gap years, the trumpet's very much... tends to be an ensemble instrument, so if the institutions aren't there for you to play with, then it's easy for it to just gather dust. And so that had been the case, and then I didn't really... I brought it with me to university last year but didn't really do anything, it just sat under my bed. And then this year as part of that whole kind of initiative to just do more stuff, just be a bit more proactive etcetera, following that third interview, I just had to.

Interviewer: So the *Paired Peers* had its impact.

Oscar: Yeah, well I just felt so bad, I had such a desolate weekly timetable, yeah so I auditioned in January for the university big band and got in. And that's been great, playing in the concert hall on Saturday.

Oscar demonstrates middle-class anxiety about the need to keep moving on, which reflects a neoliberal discourse of self-improvement (Lawler 2008). On top of joining the university big band orchestra, he was elected for a post within the Student Union, and later became actively involved in a campaign to save one of the departments in the university. Oscar, unlike Francesca, was not mobilizing his capital for employability purposes; rather, he appeared to pursue the things that interested and motivated him, but still with a sense of marking himself out. Despite the habitus interruption (Ingram and Abrahams 2016) caused by being in a world that is not theirs, both students survived by continuing to propel themselves forward.

CONCLUDING COMMENTS

This chapter has used the analogy of a 'fish out of water' to consider how working-class and middle-class students experience belonging at each of the universities in our study. We found that, at both UWE and UoB, expected norms had an impact on which students felt like a 'fish in water' and which felt like a 'fish out of water'. The implicit collusion between students who had been socialized in the same way defined acceptable ways of thinking, being, and acting within the university space. Bourdieu argues that:

> This collusion, an immediate agreement in ways of judging and acting which does not presuppose either the communication of consciousnesses, still less a contractual decision, is the basis of a practical mutual understanding, the paradigm of which might be the one established between members of a team, or, despite the antagonism, all the players engaged in a game. (Bourdieu 2000, p. 145)

This collusion ensured that at UoB, the middle-classes felt like 'fish in water', whereas some of the working-classes were fish out of water. These 'fish out of water', whilst engaged in the same game of HE, had to work harder to be included and recognized as players. UWE's more socially mixed intake arguably ensured a greater sense of fit for both classes. However, at UWE the upper fractions of the middle-classes struggled to belong. The fish out of water found different ways to navigate their way in both universities but the middle-class students at UWE had the advantage of drawing upon and mobilizing their cultural, social, and economic capital to protect their social position and to ensure that they avoided downward social mobility. These processes included gaining distinction in ways other than academic performance.

University is an important life-stage for those young people who are lucky enough to have the opportunity to participate. It can be viewed as a protected transition into adulthood and, for many, particularly those from more advantaged backgrounds, it is the first step toward becoming independent. Even though the young people in our study were aware of the harshness of graduate recruitment and employment markets, they remained positive about their futures throughout the course of their studies, seemingly believing that they would somehow be immune to graduate unemployment. But even when working-class students participate and achieve broadly similar results to middle-class students, this apparent equity disguises some of the distinction-bearing processes impacting on the degree generation which ensure that class inequalities are reinforced through the wider aspects of the student experience.

What many of the participants in our study said time and time again was that 'a degree is not enough'. There was a general understanding amongst the cohort that in order to prepare themselves for post-university employment, they needed to do more than gain a qualification. When a degree is not enough, what takes place outside of formal learning becomes highly significant. For in HE, perhaps to a greater extent than has existed in the past, the student experience has become a formalized process of capital accumulation and the means to maintain differentiation and advantage. Very often, the activities that made up the student experience amongst participants in our study served the extra purpose of allowing the development of the CV. While many students connected the wider student experience to personal development and growth, they were also attuned to thinking strategically about CV enhancement and resourcing the self for the purposes of employability. However, merely recognizing the value of engaging in CV-building activities alongside formal study did not translate directly into a take up of capital building activities. We discerned differences in access and approaches to capital building according to social class.

Overall, the working-class students were often disadvantaged when it came to mobilizing capitals to improve employment prospects. In particular, their families, whilst supportive and willing to help, did not have access to privileged and valued social capital, as well as having less economic capital, creating an uneven playing field where middle-class students were much better positioned to appropriate the stakes of the game (Bourdieu 1990). University thus does not necessarily become a social leveller; rather, it becomes another site where the middle-classes may compound and exploit their advantages.

CHAPTER 6

Getting Out

I didn't used to have any thoughts about jobs because I didn't want to think about it because I find it terrifying. Now …I guess I'm more ready to accept working. And I think I've always just dreamed of being like a rock star or something, so it's like more realistic expectations. (Lloyd, middle-class, UWE)

I have a plan of what I will do. After I finish, I think I'm going to move back home, get some kind of a temporary part-time job, even like working in a shop or something, like really menial. I'm going to then start looking for jobs and thinking about what I actually do want to do career-wise. (Lauren, middle-class, UoB)

INTRODUCTION

In the last ten years or so, there has been a lot of talk about a 'lost generation' of young people, who are denied the opportunities faced by their parents and whose aspirations to a decent lifestyle and secure employment are being stifled. Journalists Howker and Malik (2010), who coined the alternative term 'jilted generation,' and former Conservative Higher Education minister Willetts (2010) have put this down to the selfishness of the baby boom generation, clinging on to their privilege and affluence and refusing to give up their share of the social cake through higher taxes and other policies to redistribute wealth. There has also been talk in the press of a relatively new phenomenon, the 'graduate without a future' (Mason 2012), although the figures from the DeLHE surveys discussed in Chapter 1 belie this.

© The Editor(s) (if applicable) and The Author(s) 2016
A.M. Bathmaker et al., *Higher Education, Social Class and Social Mobility*, DOI 10.1057/978-1-137-53481-1_6

However, the Future Track study (Purcell et al. 2013) has demonstrated that with the increased numbers now entering HE many graduates will no longer be able to access what they describe as 'traditional graduate jobs' in the professions such as law, accountancy and the civil service; instead they may find employment in 'new graduate jobs' such as IT, web design, event organizing, and personal services. A minority may end up in non-graduate jobs in retail, hospitality work or call centres. The 2015 Green Paper on higher education estimates that 20 % of recent graduates are in such non-graduate jobs (BIS 2015). This analysis is supported by the work of Phil Brown and colleagues, who have written about the over-supply of graduates and the 'opportunity trap' they face: having accumulated considerable levels of debt to pursue their studies, they enter a hyper-competitive recruitment system and may find that their investment in a degree does not pay off (Brown 2003; Brown et al. 2011). Globalization of the labour market also means young graduates find themselves in competition with their overseas peers, who may be deemed by employers to be more 'work-ready' than the British (Brown et al. 2011). A recent survey of students and graduates in 14 countries suggested that undergraduates in the UK, South Africa and Australia are over optimistic about their preparedness for work when their views about skills offered by their courses are contrasted with the opinions of graduates actually in work (Instructure 2015).

So how did this rather bleak picture impact upon the participants in the *Paired Peers* project as they came to the end of their third year in the project? When looking back over the last year of their studies, a considerable number of the students described how stressed and overwhelmed they had been, especially coming up to their final exams. As well as completing third-year assignments, including dissertations, and revising for their all-important final examinations, they had to be thinking about where they were going to be living the following year, what they wanted to be doing and, of course, applying for jobs.

It can be argued that final-year students have always had to grapple with these competing demands on their time and energies, but we believe that there are features of the current situation that increase the pressures on these young adults, above and beyond the debts they will be carrying forward with them. First, there is the spiralling cost of rented accommodation, which, as we will see, forced many students to consider returning home (much less common amongst previous generations of UK graduates). This is a particular problem for those wanting to move to London, but is also an issue for those who wanted to remain in Bristol. Second, there is the highly competitive nature of the graduate labour market. Third, there is the fact that to compete in this market, 'a degree is not enough' (Bathmaker et al. 2013; Tomlinson 2008), so ambitious undergraduates have to fit the CV-building activities discussed in Chapter 5—such as volunteering, playing in sports teams, running societies, completing work placements and internships—into their study schedules. Finally, the process of applying for jobs, particularly top jobs, has become extremely onerous. The burden of recruitment has shifted from graduate employers to the students themselves. There has been a decline in the so-called 'milk round', the recruitment fairs held at universities across the country, which some major employers no longer take part in, except at a handful of elite universities. Now, for example, to gain a position at the Financial Conduct Authority (FCA), applicants have to complete a short form, a telephone interview, an online psychometric test, a longer application form, two more sets of psychometric tests, and finally, an assessment day. It is no wonder that some of our participants, like Lauren who is quoted at the beginning of the chapter, told us that they intended to set aside the year after graduation for job searching and applications.

The demands on the current generation of graduates, then, appear more daunting than ever, though this is always a difficult time of transition—letting go the pleasures of student existence, moving out of what so many of our respondents called 'the student bubble' and confronting the reality of earning a living; moving from dreams to realism, as Lloyd described it. The difficulty is heightened, perhaps, by the contentions made by some major employers that these young people are not sufficiently work-ready. Employer representatives at a recent Westminster Forum (where academics, policymakers, civil servants and MPs meet) compared British graduates unfavourably to overseas candidates, arguing that they displayed lesser understanding of the practices of the business world than their international counterparts. The 2015 HE Green Paper also reports that employers complain that new graduates are not 'job-ready' (BIS 2015).

This may in part be because the British education system pushes participants through more quickly than in some other parts of the world, so they are younger, and perhaps more immature and less experienced. The FCA 'Situational Choice' online test, for example, asks candidates about scenarios where they are managing a team of workers, giving presentations to clients and dealing with co-workers who are not pulling their weight—hard issues for 21-year-olds to address correctly. Some of the students in our study, indeed, acknowledged their own inadequacies in terms of becoming 'employable':

So I'm just trying to make sure I'm on top of things. There's a commercial awareness aspect of it, which I'm terrible at. I think it's the university bubble. Literally anything could be happening at the moment and I wouldn't know. (Carly, middle-class, UoB)

Last year when I did that phone interview and didn't know what was going on, and they asked me questions that I thought were horrific but really were standard, sort of standard questions like 'competitors' and 'what's the difference between this job and a different job', like you should really know if that's something you're serious about. So yeah I really feel like this year I've become so much more employable. (Harvey, working-class, UoB)

In this chapter, we look at the exit strategies of the participants as they prepared to move into the labour market. We distinguish different patterns amongst the group, in terms of their progress towards the goal of a 'good job'. We explore how their situations may reflect their class backgrounds and their gender, and the use they made of the capitals they had acquired at university. We also consider the more intangible gains of attending university, seen through the students' eyes. The chapter highlights the diversity of the students' expectations and aspirations as they set out on the next stage of their life journey.

CLASS, GENDER AND GRADUATE DESTINATIONS

In terms of their degree results, 53 participants provided information, as shown in Table 6.1. The majority (48) of both working-class and middle-class students achieved a 1st class or a 2:1. However, a greater number of middle-class students achieved a 1st, and a higher number of working-class students were awarded a 2:1.

Table 6.1 Degree results of participants in the *Paired Peers* project by social class

Degree classification	UWE working-class	UWE middle-class	UoB working-class	UoB middle-class	Total
1st	3	4	3	9	18
2:1	6	4	14	6	30
2:2	0	3	1	0	4
3rd	0	0	0	1	1
Merit	1	0	0	0	1
Total	10	11	18	16	53

Since we do not have a complete picture of the final results of our whole sample of 70 these figures must be viewed with some caution. We can suggest, however, that while universities offer a degree of equalization in terms of the acquisition of educational capital, middle-class cultural and economic capital still lend an advantage to middle-class students in terms of their academic achievements.

If we conceive of the transition from education to work as part of a life journey, it is clear that as they leave university, individuals will be positioned at different points along the road, and will have different opportunities and constraints affecting their progress on that journey. Those who did very well in their courses are likely to find it easier to move into desirable jobs than those who achieved lower grades. Those taking more vocational courses may be further on towards establishing a career path than others. Some will have family circumstances which tie them to certain locations, others are free to move wherever they may wish, or an opportunity presents itself. Some have economic resources to draw on to enable them to enter immediately into further study, others need to earn first, in order to fund Masters level or further study. Some have a clear idea of what they would like their future lives to be like, while others have no idea. Our set of students were no different. Table 6.2 shows what each student said about their intended destination at the time of the sixth interview which took place towards the end of their third year of study. The table shows the variability of destinations, across both universities and class groupings.

While each student was moving along a separate trajectory, we have grouped them into four broad clusters, leaving aside the nine students who were going on to a final (fourth) year of undergraduate study. Some already had a destination set up (a course, a job, an internship). We define these as being 'on track'. Others did not yet have a confirmed destination, but they had a fairly clear idea of where they wanted to go and were taking steps to get there, for example, they were applying for jobs or placements in the occupations in which they wished to work. We have labelled these as 'pushing forward'. A third cluster consisted of people who had decided they needed some kind of break before moving on to a career. Some of these had been offered jobs or places on courses, but had postponed taking them up. We refer to this group as having 'deferred careers'. Finally, there was a group who had very little idea of what they wanted to do, or how to go about it, or who harboured rather vague ambitions: we have categorized them as 'drifters'. This is summarized in Table 6.3, which

Table 6.2 Intended destinations of final-year undergraduates when interviewed in the summer of 2013 arranged by university and class

Name	Intended destination
University of Bristol Middle-class	
Adrian	Masters in economics
Carly	Seeking a job in accountancy
Cerys	Looking for bar work or equivalent. Longer term interest in social work
Craig	Fourth year engineering
David	Law conversion, then Legal Practice Course (LPC)
Elliot	Masters in English. Hoping to be an academic or journalist
Farrah	Law conversion, aiming for LPC solicitor
Hannah	Has applied for a medical degree
Harry	Nothing fixed, interested in social housing, possibly Masters in social policy
Jenifer	Fourth year in engineering
Lauren	No idea
Liam	Applying for city/management consultancy jobs
Luke	Assistant in father's yacht hire firm
Martha	No job. Interest in sustainability
Martin	No job. Interest in charity/voluntary sector
Max	No job. Hopes to go to drama school
Nathan	Merchant Bank
Rose	Placement at a children's theatre
Sally	PGCE
Scarlett	PGCE, primary teaching, special needs
Sebastian	Finance sector internship
University of Bristol Working-class	
Anna	PGCE
Amelia	No job. Wants to do something to do with biology
Bianca	Law conversion—had chance of a training contract but felt she needed a break. Worked in law firm as summer job
Connie	Masters in medieval history
Freya	Ambition to work in big cat conservation, seeking research jobs abroad
Garry	Has applied to teach English in summer camp and is considering teaching
Jade	Looking for jobs, some interest in Human Resource Management (HRM)
Justin	Seeking job as a teaching assistant, hoping to do post graduate teacher training
Lizzie	Fourth year in engineering
Harvey	Interviewed for brokering job with major financial firm and has an internship fixed
Jackie	PGCE primary teaching
Nicole	Internship with a charity
Marcus	Fourth year in engineering
Megan	Has Teach First place but taking year out to work with horses
Melissa	Applying for masters. Interest in journalism

(continued)

Table 6.2   (continued)

Name	Intended destination
Samantha	Masters
Sean	Applying for graduate scheme at Department for International Development
Tony	Banking internship
Zoe	No job. Interest in media
UWE Middle-class	
Amber	Pub job at home. Fourth year engineering
Amina	Wants a gap year travelling
Anthony	No job
Christopher	Working in pub, while applying for Masters (LPC or International Relations)
Donna	Applying for finance jobs
Dylan	Unpaid internship in poll lobbying
Emma	Postgraduate Certificate in Education (PGCE)
Francesca	Working in restaurant for year while applying for law jobs
Harriet	No job
Jeff	Retaking final year
Jessica	No job
Joanna	Seeking role with police in child protection. Secured place teaching in Thailand
Lilly	Working for church
Lloyd	No job, seeking internships, interested in music journalism
Lynn	Masters in Theatre studies. Working for a company
Nicholas	Fourth year engineering
Oscar	No job
UWE Working-class	
Abigail	Fourth year in economics and finance
Adele	No job. Interest in charity/voluntary sector
Charlie	No job. Seeking work in finance
Jasmine	Taking year off, then doing Masters in Social Work
Keren	Job at restaurant, before moving on to apply for teaching
Kyle	Resitting one module, ambition to be a barrister
Leo	Looking for jobs in finance
Miles	No job. Worked in landscape gardening. Something outdoor or Masters
Rob	Fourth year engineering
Ruby	PGCE primary
Sariah	No job Planning to go to America and work in fashion
Shane	Fourth year on placement at present, wants to be a chartered accountant
Sophie	Wants to work for council, applying for jobs

Table 6.3   Intended destinations by university and class of origin

	UoB middle-class	UoB working-class	UWE middle-class	UWE working-class	Totals
Further study	7	5	2	1	15
On track	4	3	1	0	8
Pushing forward	2	2	3	3	10
Drifting	5	4	8	3	20
Deferred career	1	3	1	3	8
Final 4th year study	2	2	3	3	9
Totals	21	19	17	13	70

shows how the students from the two universities were clustered in terms of their class background as well as the university they attended. We distinguish here between the two 'on track' groups, those going to further study and those going into the labour market.

It is worth mentioning that, in a previous research study carried out in the early 2000s amongst young adults aged 20–34 living in Bristol, a significant proportion within this wider age group were categorized as drifters (Bradley and Devadason 2008). This study, entitled *Winners and Losers* and funded by the Economic and Social Research Council (ESRC), showed that even in their 30s, many young adults were unsure of their occupational destinations. It was argued at the time that the changing nature of the labour market, even before the onset of world recession in 2007–2008, was making it hard for young adults to settle into secure employment. We were observing a world in which many were being trapped within a low-wage economy, in more precarious employment where the 'job for life' was becoming a thing of the past. They might be seen as part of the evolving class of the 'precariat', the international phenomenon identified by Standing (2011) as produced by the processes of economic globalization and neo-liberalism: a huge body of workers in insecure, transient and informal forms of employment. The result for young people is an ever-lengthening transition to adult independence, and a fracturing of traditional career paths.

Tables 6.2 and 6.3 both suggest that there is an institutional effect, and class differences are strongly mediated by university attended. The most striking feature is that those who attended UoB, whatever their class, were making a speedier and smoother transition into work. This is a crucial finding in terms of the debates over widening participation and social mobility. It suggests that attending a Russell Group university does indeed heighten the chances for working-class students of upward mobility and securing professional employment, while for middle-class students it is likely to help them maintain their status. While UWE has a strong record of getting its graduates into employment, it may be that they will take longer to find a niche, or indeed end up in non-graduate jobs: it is too early at this stage to be certain, but we can say that the graduates from UoB in our study had a head start.

How has this been achieved? We suggest that the working-class people who succeed in gaining a place at UoB were highly motivated and determined to achieve. They were more likely to learn how to play the game. Thus we saw how Harvey learned how to be more employable as he went through his career. Extremely instrumental from the start of his degree (he often mentioned how boring he found economics) he was able to build up social capital through his friendship with middle-class students, including the son of a wealthy rock star. His sporting ability (at golf and football) and his entrepreneurial streak (market trading, selling wine to his fellows) were experiential assets from his working-class background that he could add to the capitals gained from university. Tony, also working-class and headed for the City, had also quickly learned how to play the strategic game.

Some working-class students were making use of their gains in cultural capital and proceeding to masters degrees or PGCE teaching qualifications, with ambitions to pursue careers as teachers or academics. These students had achieved well academically, gaining a first-class degree or a 2.1 classification. As discussed in Chapter 4, a lack of advantage ensures that drive and determination are needed for working-class educational success, which arguably made many predisposed to work harder than their middle-class and public school counterparts, a finding replicating the much earlier research of Brown and Scase (1994), which was discussed in Chapter 1.

Perhaps more surprising, however, is that middle-class students were more likely to end up in our category of drifters (13 middle-class compared with 7 working-class). This perhaps reflects the fact that going to university has become a middle-class norm, whether or not young people have formed career plans. It can be argued, as well, that as their parents are more able to support them financially, they are under less pressure to get a job and become independent. The working-class students who were not yet 'on track' were more likely to have some idea of where they wanted to go, although it might take them longer to get there, for example, by taking non-graduate work in order to save up for a masters. However, the phenomenon of middle-class drifting may also reflect a real decline in middle-class fortunes, as public-sector jobs which past cohorts were able to access are lost.

Clearly, it is too early as yet to make any firm statements about the impact of university on graduates' experience of social mobility. However, the relatively good prospects of the working-class participants at UoB suggest that for some, at least, it may remain a vehicle for upward mobility into professional status. The next phase of our research, which is exploring the career paths of our cohort over the next four years, will reveal whether this prediction is accurate.

Gender Differences in Students' Initial Choices and Destinations

Analysis of the students' destinations also suggest that career outcomes for graduates are more shaped by gender than class, as is shown in Table 6.4. While at the outset of our research we observed little difference in the aspirations and expectations of our female and male undergraduates, over the three years there appeared to be some kind of cooling out process where the horizons of women participants contracted. Young women who started off saying they wanted to be barristers lowered their horizons to being solicitors. This is also reflected in the higher number of women who were drifting or deferring careers, as shown in Table 6.4.

Also notable was a tendency amongst a number of the women in our study to head towards teaching. The table shows that women were more likely to go on to further study than men. Six of these 12 women were taking a Post-Graduate Certificate in Education (a one-year graduate

Table 6.4 Student destinations by university and gender

	UoB males	UoB females	UWE males	UWE females	Totals
Further study	3	9	0	3	15
On track jobs	5	2	0	1	8
Moving on	2	2	3	3	10
Drifting	3	6	4	7	20
Deferred career	2	2	1	3	8
Final year	2	2	4	1	9
Totals	17	23	11	18	70

teaching qualification). None of the men were doing so, although two were considering it as a future option.

Some young women came to university intending to teach. Three of these were the children of teachers. Always seen as an appropriate job for women, it is perhaps not coincidental that it appears more compatible with motherhood, because the hours and holidays coincide with children's. Perhaps naively, the young women assumed that it would be a less pressurized environment than the traditional male-dominated professions of engineering, law and merchant banking. Anna, who was very keen to do something with her politics degree to challenge injustices and inequalities, found the behaviour of male students and tutors daunting, and decided that her best contribution would be to teach maths to children in disadvantaged areas. She was bitterly disappointed not to be selected for the Teach First programme, which places bright young applicants directly into schools where their skills are needed, but settled for a PGCE and was looking forward to it.

The most striking case, however, was that of Sally, a middle-class student studying law at UoB. Sally stood out from the rest of the students, as she was the only one with a child. This obviously placed constraints on her, but she was able to dedicate herself to her studies as she lived at home and had both childcare and financial help from her parents. Sally seemed typically ambitious, with a strong desire to be a barrister, following a pathway set out for her with strong parental endorsement. In her second year, she had decided being a solicitor would be her preference: 'I'm doing a law degree so I'll be a lawyer.' But doubts began to set in during her third year:

> I think I still want to be a solicitor but it's just really hard to be a solicitor. You have to work really long hours and things like that, so it's not a particularly practical route to go down. Because I was thinking for a while over summer about teaching.

Sally decided that the legal profession was too competitive and demanding for her, especially as a lone parent. She had seen how lawyer friends of her parents worked long hours and then brought work home. So she decided to switch to teaching.

> Because I think I would much prefer to teach and then maybe be able to teach Law than have the stresses of having to practise it as a profession. Because everyone seems so stressed about it, all the lawyers that I know who

live on my road, they're all up at 3 in the morning ringing China every day and it just doesn't...like the more I think about it the less it appeals to me.

This cost her some psychological heartache, as she felt she was letting her parents down:

> My stepdad's like a self-employed sort of electronics fiddly around person, my mum's a nurse for the NHS, and so they were boasting "oh my daughter's doing a law degree, she's going to be this hot-shot solicitor, it's going to be amazing", and then I just came home and I was like "I'm going to be a teacher". And they were like "Really? You're not going to be a lawyer?" "Nope". And for months and months they were there, researching online, going "I'm sure if you do the LPC [Legal Practice Course] you can get this job." "I'm sure you can probably get a training contract in a few years' time after you do this." And things like that. I was like "No, I've made up my mind, I just can't." So that was tricky.

However, she maintained her middle-class high-achieving view of her potential career path. In contrast to Jackie, a working-class student also at UoB and progressing to a PGCE, who said, 'I'm not particularly interested in being head teacher or deputy or anything, like senior member of staff', Sally explained:

> I don't see being a teacher as like what I'm going to do for ever. I feel like I could do a lot more than just being a teacher. After maybe 2 years as a teacher, so in like 3 years' time, I would have started thinking about trying to go for Head of Department or an external examiner for something, or something a bit different. I feel like being a teacher is just like a stepping stone to something bigger and more elaborate, but I haven't worked out what it is yet.

While Jackie anticipated a steady career, Sally's middle-class perspective led her to aim if not to be a 'hotshot lawyer' at least to be a 'hotshot teacher'.

On Track: Moving on Up

Many of those we categorized as being 'on track' had known from the start of the degree what they wanted to do, and had chosen courses which would lead them towards that destination. Throughout their degrees, they had carefully planned the next stages in the passage towards that desired goal, continuing a personal strategic stance of planning which could be seen when they entered university, as discussed in Chapter 4. Such a one was Tony, who was studying economics at Bristol:

> It's gone the way that I wanted it to go actually, get an internship, get a graduate role, go straight into work. I'm open to it changing but it's gone exactly the way I hoped it would to start with...I think I can kind of rise quite well within the industry. It's what I like so if it's what I like I'd assume that I can at least kind of motivate myself to do it well. Yeah I'm reasonably confident. I think a bit of confidence will probably help. (Tony, middle-class, UoB)

Another who had planned everything carefully was Nathan, a middle-class law student at Bristol, who throughout his degree had been remarkably focused on obtaining his goal of a very well paid job in the City. In a blog he posted in his second year, he had expressed a degree of contempt for his fellow students who did not seem to be applying themselves wholeheartedly to their studies or taking advantage of the chances being offered them. By contrast, he was doing everything he could to get the high-status career he aspired to:

> Get exposed to the companies and the industries that you might want to work for as early as possible. Research the opportunities available, (which I did), and summer internships (which I did and got the job off the back off). Join societies and clubs and try and take up leadership positions in those clubs that are relevant to the potential career that you want—if the society doesn't exist, create it. [...] Just try and do everything to build up your CV, just add little bits of experience, add little bits of training, competitions if you can, and make yourself look busy.

Highly intelligent and by his own account 'driven', Nathan had come to university well prepared for the game, and had started quickly to accumulate cultural and social capital; as we shall see later in the chapter, he did not take a wholly instrumental view of his studies, but he knew what he wanted and was taking the appropriate steps to get there:

> I was quite driven from the go, and I think I probably still am, and I just refined where exactly I was going to go in the City. Because originally I'd been thinking maybe work for a FTSE firm, maybe work for a law firm. I did law because it was a good degree, rather than because I wanted to be a lawyer.

> So now I have to refine that to finance and a particular area within finance, so I don't really think it's changed much. (Nathan, middle-class, UoB)

Nathan got a first-class degree, adding high educational capital to his portfolio, and gained a place at a leading merchant bank, which would start him off on a high salary. He was clearly able to maximize a range of capitals and put them to work while at university, thus setting him on the route to a high-flying career.

Pushing Forward: Progress Towards a Goal

> I'm looking for like graduate schemes at home, so like with the councils. But because I've got my job I can leave it a bit because I can live on my wages at the moment because I'll be moving back home. But I think I need to focus more on getting the grades first rather than looking for jobs because I could apply like in the summer, so I'm panicking a bit because I want to try and find something now, but I think I should get the grades first and then look for jobs. (Sophie, working-class, UWE)

As we have indicated, many of the students found the final year of their degree very stressful, especially the run up to the all-important final assessments. Some who had quite clear ideas of what they would like to do had not managed as yet to line up a placement or a job, but had some kind of a plan for the year ahead.

Sophie illustrates the trend we have identified amongst a number of young women of modifying their ambitions, but her interviews make clear how her horizons for action were also marked by a class habitus, right from the point of selecting universities that would be appropriate for her. Sophie came from a working-class family living in a town near Bristol and was studying Politics and International Studies at UWE. The first in her family to go to university, she spoke very tellingly of her motivation in applying to UWE:

> I didn't really want to choose universities that were too high, I wanted to become like my level, I didn't want to aim **above my station**, so I only applied for three places, like here, Aston and Coventry.

Despite this indication of sensing how she was positioned in the class order, when she was interviewed in the first year she spoke of her interest in the civil service, foreign office or diplomatic service, partly perhaps because she was keen to make her parents proud of her achievements. But these are, of course, very competitive areas to access, which seemed at odds with Sophie's own account of her personality: 'I don't like to fail, I like to be comfortable'. It is not then, perhaps, so surprising that by the second year, she was considering working in the voluntary sector, and then what seemed a more achievable goal of a local council job in her home town, especially as she had a relative working there. In her final interview, she appeared quite composed about her next moves. Her plan (which was fairly typical of this cluster) was to have a holiday, 'relax a bit', and then move back home to her parents and start looking for a job. She had, in fact, already started on this process, although it had not yielded a result:

> I've contacted the council regarding jobs that they've put on the website already, saying that if I applied and get the job would you keep it until I finish, but the ones at the moment have said no, they need them straightaway, which is fair enough. But if I keep asking them, eventually something will turn up.

Leo was another working-class student who had nothing fixed at the end of his three years. He had left school and gone straight into work in an accountancy office, which he had found boring and which had motivated him to go to university, especially as he perceived that his friends who were students were having a 'good time'; indeed this seemed to be mainly what he was seeking from his student experience. He anticipated ending up in some kind of office work, but had not succeeded in his second year at getting a paid internship, nor could he afford an unpaid one. Unlike Nathan and Tony whose cases were discussed above he did not seem to have grasped the need to prepare himself for the labour of acquiring a good job, which was more familiar to middle-class students. Moreover, the experience of completing applications seemed to have been discouraging:

> National Grid, I first of all got a refusal because I did an online test, like a rejection, then they e-mailed me later saying that they had adjusted the boundaries and I'm back in—but I still haven't heard anything back...it would be good to try and get. But the applications, they're so lengthy, it's really frustrating.

We initially viewed Leo as a drifter because of a distinctly laid-back orientation to HE study. Asked to describe the 'typical student', he stated 'lazy' and confessed that there was something of that in him: 'I can motivate myself when I want to, but a lot of the time I choose not to.' At the same time, he appeared to work pretty steadily at his Economics and Finance degree at UWE and had obtained some first-class marks. By the end of his final year, he was expecting to go home and continue his efforts to get on to a graduate scheme:

> I've only applied for two, and got turned down for one, still waiting on the other one, but yeah I haven't really put as much effort into finding a graduate scheme as I should have. But that's what I'm hoping to do. I'm applying to go anywhere over the country, usually in the finance departments for large businesses. It looks like at the minute I'll probably have to move back to [home town] for a while.

Leo and Sophie probably typify a subset of students with moderate ambitions who, during the course of their degree, decide on a course of action which is realistic in terms of their qualifications and achievements but who are not driven in the same way as some of the high-fliers. Moreover, if working-class students succeed in getting this type of middle-of-the-road job, they may be considered to have done well in the eyes of their parents and their own reference groups, whose expectations are not set as high as the middle-class parents of students like Nathan and Sally. These working-class students are focused on employment and have aspirations, but these are framed in a more limited way that reflects both their class habitus and their realistic grasp of their more limited stock of capitals.

Deferred Career: Time for a Break

As we have stressed above, many of the students, particularly the young women, found the final year of their degree very stressful and draining. Thus a few of those who had a plan for their destination or had actually achieved a job or place on a course that would lead towards a graduate career had decided that they needed a period of recovery before stepping onwards. This might be presented as a need for a break from long years of intensive engagement with education, especially for those from working-class backgrounds who had not been able to afford the more glamorous type of gap year prior to starting university. Jasmine was aiming to be a social worker, but told us of her need for a break:

I was going to go straight into a masters, but I want a year out, to save up, get a flat and stuff. Cos I just can't cope. So I'm moving in with my boyfriend. (Jasmine, working-class, UWE)

The lure of travelling, with cheap flights, schemes such as Eurorail/ Eurail and the almost universal availability of bar work, was strong for some of the students. One such was Megan, a forceful and determined young woman from a working-class background who wanted to teach, but was seizing the chance to fulfil her passion for horses and riding. She had gained a place on the Teach First programme—an achievement, as it is highly competitive—but had decided to defer it for a year:

I've deferred it so I'm having a year out. One thing I will do is the four months in Canada. There's a Work Away placement where I would work with training young horses on a ranch, which is my dream ... And because it's Work Away I work at their ranch for four to six hours a day and they pay for my food and board, so I don't pay for any of that so it will be quite cheap. There's another horse-related thing I really want to do, which is a project where you live and ride with Mongolian nomadic people for a month. And if anyone is the best riders, Mongolian riders are the ones to watch, they're just phenomenal. And so you'd live in a traditional round tent called a ger and you'd travel across Mongolia with them, which would be phenomenal. But it's expensive, so we'll see. (Megan, working-class, UoB)

Drifting: What Shall I Do with My Life?

A common phrase used by the respondents in the *Winners and Losers* research mentioned earlier in the chapter was 'sorting my life out'. Given the young age of most graduates (typically 21–23) and their lack of experience with the wider world and its opportunities, it is not surprising that there was a group of young people who were unclear about what they wanted from the future. Although universities do their best to orient their students towards the labour market—UWE brands itself 'The University for the Real World'—given the absorbing nature of student culture and study, many students put off the crucial life decisions, concentrating on the here and now while they are studying. This may not be so irrational. As one of the students whom we classified as a drifter put it:

I don't really see the point in making longer term goals because you don't know what's going to happen, stuff might change. (Donna, middle-class, UWE)

For those who have not formed in their teenage years any idea of a career they wanted to pursue, it becomes more an instance of serendipity—of seeing what is out there. Realistically, some of the drifters knew that they were likely to change over the coming years, as Lauren (middle-class, UoB) explained:

> I'm not going to initially start looking for a career as soon as I've done my exams because I don't think that's practical, I don't think that's realistic, so I think it will take time...This sounds really like pessimistic or weird, but I can't see myself in the future. I try and like think about what will I be like in like 5 or 10 years and I just...I can't vision anything, I just can't imagine it.

This proposal to spend some time exploring possibilities was often accompanied by a decision to return home, and to continue with jobs in bars or restaurants taken up during or before the study period. This may, perhaps, be seen as a move to bring a degree of stability and security in a precarious and shifting world. It also illustrates the importance of their families to these young people, and the ways in which family resources enable or constrain how students envisage their next steps on graduation, as stressed in former chapters. Many of these drifters were from middle-class families who would be able to support them and offer necessary resources (such as funding for further study or training) while they were 'sorting out' what they wanted to do:

> I'll probably just move back home and I have a job at a pub at home, and I do invigilating at my old school, so that will sort of get me started for a month or so, and then hopefully in that time I will be able to find a job for either starting in September or starting in the summer, really just for a year, and then hopefully within that year I'll maybe do some work experience in different sectors and see what sort of thing I fancy going into. I've not decided on anything yet. Just try and get some work experience in different areas. (Amber, middle-class, UWE)

As Tables 6.3 and 6.4 show, we identified drifters from both universities and all classes, although male students from both classes at UoB were least likely to drift. It may be the case, however, that some working-class students end up as drifters not because of indecisiveness, as displayed by middle-class graduates Amber and Lauren, but because they lack insider knowledge of the professional world and its cultural and social parameters. They do not come to university with the cultural capital that middle-class students possess. They have no maps of this terrain to guide them. They lack the safety nets provided by families with ample resources.

An interesting example of this was Miles, a young man from South Wales who we identified as working-class, despite his own evasiveness about class identification. Miles, who studied geography at UWE, might be seen as a typical sort of carefree student. He told us how much he loved Bristol and had apparently enjoyed his three years of student life, though he feared he might be heading for a 2:2 degree outcome. However, his account seemed to indicate continuing attachment to what might be called a working-class worldview; respect for practical rather than bureaucratic skills, a pragmatic acceptance of what life may offer, a trust in fate and luck. Thus, he appeared rather contemptuous of his student peers, comparing them unfavourably with his friends back in Wales, in the same way that we saw in Chapter 5 that Marcus viewed his middle-class flatmates:

Miles had worked for a landscape gardening company until it folded, spoke of wanting to work outdoors, of not wanting a boring job, and seemed unconcerned about his own lack of direction, stating that he expected to find work in Bristol, even if it was only labouring.

> But I'm not worried about the future. It does concern me what's going to happen but there's no point worrying about it. As my dad said, don't worry about it, everything will work out one way or another.

Miles offers an interesting insight as to how moving towards middle-class occupational status does not necessarily bring with it an abandonment of original class habitus. In terms of individual social mobility this may prove a hindrance, but if our interest in mobility is more to do with breaking down the sharp divisions in the valuing of class milieux and habitus, and with overcoming the stigmatization of the working classes described so vividly by writers like Jones (2011) and McKenzie (2015), then we may need more like Miles to mix things up.

Value Added? What Students Take Out with Them

So far, we have discussed the career or educational destinations that our cohort of students were set for as they left university. But it is important not to give the impression that the whole purpose of university is getting a job. To do so would be to accept an instrumentalist, neo-liberal and market-oriented ideology of HE, which has unfortunately been embraced by too many vice-chancellors and their management teams, albeit under the whip of successive government policies. Going to university is, still, about far more than building a career. It is also about enrichment, maturation, the expanding of horizons and a developing depth of understanding of one's chosen discipline.

Nathan, for example, who, as we have seen was a very serious and committed student, commented on the intellectual enlargement that had resulted from his law degree:

> I think it's incredibly difficult and incredibly rewarding. If you start to question absolutely everything that you see, you start to question the media, you start to question the press, you start to question what people say to you. You spot a bad argument and tear it to shreds. And it makes you question why, rather than just accepting things. So that's a quite abstract part. So that will be a good way of changing, it makes you more open minded and more questioning of things. (Nathan, middle-class, UoB)

For others, it was more a questioning or growing up acquiring life skills and confidence. Jasmine emphasized a whole range of gains from being a student:

> I've gained a better work ethic, I've gained knowledge of my subject, far more than I had at A level. Gained a lot of friends, gained so much independence from moving out of home and living by myself, and learning to cook things other than beans on toast, so that's good. I've gained quite a lot, I just feel much more confident about now and the future. I've gained that from uni as well. (Jasmine, working-class, UWE)

For Sophie, this was specifically about developing skills and confidence that would take her to the goal of a decent stable job:

> I suppose just again confidence in going to an interview...if I got to the interview stages of a job I probably would do better now than what I did before just because I'm more confident in answers I give and things like that. I think just general confidence and happy to speak to people, which I didn't have before. (Sophie, working-class, UWE)

These quotations from two working-class students suggest that they have benefitted in various ways from the 'moratorium' (Brake 1980) which university has long offered to middle-class youths. Both talk of increased confidence; although neither has yet secured a job, these skills and the growth of maturity may help to carry them forward into the world where they must compete against those from more advantaged backgrounds and perhaps set them apart from those 'back home' who have not entered HE.

This sense of maturing, of moving towards being an adult, was commented on by many, looking back over the three years in which we had been working with them.

> I feel like I'm finally starting to feel a realistic sense of what I can achieve and what I can't achieve. That's probably a better way of putting it. Like when you're a kid you think you can do everything and like, you know, it's so idealistic, and then I went through a stage being like "oh my God I can't do anything", and now I kind of feel like I understand more what my limitations are and what I can and can't do. And so it's given me that. (Megan, working-class, UoB)

> Just general life skills in a way. Like before I came to uni I never really understood how people paid bills, or just general things that adults are supposed to do, like I never really understood any of that, and then like having gone to uni it's like it's not actually that hard. (Luke, middle-class, UoB)

> I appreciate things a bit more. I took things for granted when I was younger. Like family. Like my mum, I did take the piss a bit...She used to do everything for me—absolutely everything, wash clothes. She still does a lot—brings food. I do appreciate everything. I try to, I think I do. (Miles, working-class, UWE)

Above all there was a sense of expanded horizons, moving beyond the homogenized relationships typical of their home backgrounds, in terms both of ethnic diversity and class difference:

> Definitely going to uni opened me up to that whole different world of people like from...like the state school I went to where everyone was white, to suddenly mixing with people from all over the world is a big contrast. (Jade, working-class, UoB)

> The six of us couldn't be further apart. One of my flatmates, his dad is like filthy rich, and stuff. Big property developer from Cardiff. So there's money there. Private school, yeah, one of the best schools in Cardiff I think. But then again, there's another boy from up north, you know, who's more

similar to me, he understands the meaning, the value of stuff, a lot more. I get along with him the best. He's funny. And then there's like, people from—one boy is from Hastings, who's sort of... completely, completely different way of life again. It's good—it's an eye opener. (Miles, working-class, UWE)

University does not just offer the chance of gaining a decent job or a career; it offers a deeper understanding of the world, an expansion of horizons. This is something that the majority of our participants, whatever their class origin, will carry forward with them on the next stage of their journey.

Concluding Comments

In 2014 the Guardian newspaper commissioned a survey of parents of secondary school children across England and Wales about the fees regime and the value of HE. The survey found that 58 % considered university education to be poor value for money and only 14 % thought that despite the fees, it was a good deal. Many parents were considering cheaper alternatives such as apprenticeships or MOOCs (online courses) for their children's futures. This is not surprising, given that the overall cost of a three-year degree (and there are quite a number of four-year courses on offer), putting together fees and living expenses, is estimated at £50,000 (Ward and Shaw 2014).

However, although we commenced this chapter by stressing the very difficult socio-economic climate which faced young people as they set out on their journeys of transition, it should be remembered that, at least in the past, there have been clear advantages in having a degree. Graduates are less likely to experience long-term unemployment. There is a very pronounced graduate pay premium. BIS figures for 2014 showed that the median average earnings for all in the 16–64 age group with postgraduate degrees is £40,000, and for graduates £31,000, compared with £22,000 for non-graduates. For those aged 21–30, the differentials are lower, with median earnings at around £28,000, £26,000 and £18,000. It is not clear whether this younger group will subsequently catch up or whether the premium is actually decreasing, as is suggested by BIS (2015). Of course, the premium will also vary according to the type of degree gained: we all know that doctors and lawyers are better paid than philosophers and drama teachers. The question, however, is whether in the current economic climate our participants will be able to harvest that premium or whether they may find themselves confined to the precariat or in non-graduate jobs.

It remains to be seen whether the difficulties facing the students in our study are a lifecycle or generational effect. Is this truly a 'lost' or a 'jilted' generation? It may be that the young adults will catch up with these higher levels over their life-time, especially as the economy picks up; on the other hand, it might be the case that, as Mason and Howker and Malik argued, that this generation may find itself trapped in a 'high-skill, low-wage' economy. Nevertheless, as the Guardian pointed out in its report (Ward and Shaw 2014), those without degrees are much more likely to find themselves unemployed. University remains a gateway into high-level professional employment, and is also something of a guarantee of calibre to recruiters and employers who can be mistrustful of young people's work ethic and capabilities.

We have argued in this chapter that this gateway is open to at least some of the young people from less-advantaged backgrounds who have the talent and grit to overcome barriers into HE. They achieve good degrees—though, in our study, more achieved 2:1s than firsts, compared with their middle-class peers. As Table 6.3 shows, they are only slightly less likely than their more advantaged peers to have secured a destination at the end of their years of study: facing a cruel and competitive labour market, the majority of graduates from both class groupings have not yet found a niche, and nor would the literature on youth transitions lead us to expect they would have (e.g. Bradley and Devadason 2008; Furlong and Cartmel 2007; Roberts 1995; Woodman and Wyn 2015). All recent research on the transition from education to employment emphasizes how transitions have become lengthened and fractured.

However, there appears from the *Paired Peers* study to be a major advantage for students of all classes if they attend an elite university like Bristol, compared to even a leading modern, post-1992 university such as UWE. In this respect, not much has changed since the Brown and Scase study of 1994. We find this deeply disappointing. In our view, the blame must fall upon employers and recruiters who focus so narrowly on a handful of 'top' universities and do not widen their search for talent into newer arenas. Nonetheless, if we consider the role of universities in offering social mobility to talented working-class young people, there is evidence here to suggest that this role continues. The problem is that far fewer people from working-class backgrounds make it to university and, when they do, they are over-represented in the less 'prestigious' universities.

This is a systemic problem that will not be addressed by letting a few more working-class young people into elite universities.

There is a gender issue, too. Some of the young women seemed to drift away from original ambitions to be lawyers, engineers, politicians, and employees of elite city firms. Young women like Sally and Isabel began to question whether they wanted to engage in the competitive environments into which they were being inducted. Teaching appears to offer the advantage of greater compatibility with raising children. There are attitude differences too. Women asked about the kind of job they wanted were more likely to talk about working with people, or about 'giving something back' or 'making a difference' while young men were more likely to talk of money and status. It seems that the ideology associated with the patriarchal concept of the 'male breadwinner' dies hard.

Meanwhile, the cohort of young graduates in our study did not seem too daunted as they set forth on their journey to adult independence. We might describe their mood as apprehensive but hopeful. Some were already on the way to traditional graduate employment, as accountants, lawyers, teachers and engineers. Others were resigned to starting out in 'non-graduate' jobs, while they took further steps to better their chances, for example, by applying to graduate-entry schemes. Finally, some appeared quite directionless, with no real idea of how their lives might turn out. Many of them will remain dependent on their parents for a while, returning to live at home while finding their feet, joining the growing proportion of young adults who continue to live at home. Indeed, in the face of recession and austerity, links with the family may be becoming strengthened, in chains of economic and emotional interdependence.

Whatever their place on the road to the future, participants had few regrets about the choice they had made to attend university. When we asked if they would still have opted for university if they had been required to pay the £9000 annual fees introduced the year after they started, the majority said they would have done so, though some of the working-class students suggested they might have chosen a more vocationally oriented course, with a clearer line of sight to a specific field of employment. But even if they had not yet discerned a route to collect the economic rewards they had hoped a degree would bring, most of them acknowledged the pleasures—intellectual, social and cultural—which their student experience had brought them. A degree may not be enough, but most of this 'degree generation' believed it to be essential.

CHAPTER 7

Narratives of Class and 'Race'

Over the past three years people have said things about race. Not negative things. Just like "oh she's the Black one". So I guess in a way, being a different race does change things. Sometimes you will be sitting in a room and notice that you're the only person that's not white. (Nicole, UoB, working-class, mixed heritage Black)

I don't notice that I'm white, and I don't notice that I'm middle-class. (Sally, UoB, middle-class, white)

Interviewer: OK, and how has your own class, gender and ethnicity affected your experience of university?

Liam: It hasn't. I'm white, middle class, fully British back as far as the 12th century or whatever, it's not affected me at all. (Liam, UoB, middle-class, white)

INTRODUCTION

Previous chapters have shown how social class contributes to the production of students' dispositions, practices and horizons for action in HE. While the central focus of our study is social class, this chapter extends the analysis to explore ways in which class intersects with race, recognizing that 'class factors articulate with 'race' and ethnicity to produce complex patterns of participation in higher education' (Brah and Phoenix 2004, p. 82).

© The Editor(s) (if applicable) and The Author(s) 2016
A.M. Bathmaker et al., *Higher Education, Social Class and Social Mobility*, DOI 10.1057/978-1-137-53481-1_7

The way that class works in complex and contradictory ways, for both middle-class and working-class Black, Asian and Minority Ethnic (BAME) populations in England, has become a focus of increasing attention in research (e.g. Archer 2011; Basit 2013; Reay 2008; Reay et al. 2005; Rollock et al. 2015; Shah et al. 2010; Wallace 2016). This work draws on theories of intersectionality that direct attention to how axes of differentiation work together to create specific conditions of disadvantage (or advantage). Following on from Crenshaw's (1989, 1991) work in the USA in the 1990s, Brah and Phoenix (2004, p. 75) have argued that studying the intersection of class, gender and ethnicity 'allows a more complex and dynamic understanding than a focus on social class alone'. Brah and Phoenix define intersectionality as follows:

> We regard the concept of 'intersectionality' as signifying the complex, irreducible, varied, and variable effects which ensue when multiple axes of differentiation—economic, political, cultural, psychic, subjective and experiential—intersect in historically specific contexts. The concept emphasizes that different dimensions of social life cannot be separated out into discrete and pure strands. (Brah and Phoenix 2004, p. 76)

We start this chapter by providing an overview of statistical data on Black, Asian and Minority Ethnic students, which locates the experience of students in our study against a background of continuing patterns of inequalities in HE. We then consider the largely unspoken whiteness of the HE environment in England (Clegg et al. 2003), before looking in detail at the experiences of the students from BAME backgrounds in the *Paired Peers* project. We are aware of the debates and contestation around the use of different terms to name and talk about 'race' (see Warmington 2014; Bradley 2016). We use the rather awkward term 'Black, Asian and Minority Ethnic' and its clumsy acronym BAME, because, despite its possible limitations, as a term it is inclusive of the range of different backgrounds of students in the *Paired Peers* study. Warmington (2014) convincingly argues against putting 'race' in scare quotes. Nevertheless, we have adopted the practice here, to distance ourselves from essentialist thinking. We also employ the broader term ethnicity to cover a range of identities which differ from that of the white majority. However, our participants themselves used the word 'race' in talking about their experiences, and we have therefore used it in the title of this chapter.

Black, Asian and Minority Ethnic Students in English Higher Education

Data on BAME students and HE in England present a complex picture of their experience. Participation by BAME students has increased over the past decade, and their proportion has risen from 14.9 % of all students in 2003–2004 to 19.6 % in 2012–2013, the year that students in the *Paired Peers* project completed three years of undergraduate study (Equality Challenge Unit 2014, p. 116). At first sight, this proportion appears high in comparison to the overall BAME population in the UK, which was 9 % at the time of the 2001 UK census, rising to 14 % at the 2011 census (Jivraj 2012; ONS 2012). However, the percentage of young people aged 16–24 from Black, Asian and Minority Ethnic populations is higher than in the population as a whole, and at the time of the 2011 census, 23 % of 16–24-year olds were classified as coming from a BAME background. Furthermore, participation varies across different sector or 'mission' groups. In 2012–2013, 17.8 % of students at Russell Group universities (of which the University of Bristol is a member), were from BAME backgrounds. During the same year, 20.3 % of students attending University Alliance institutions (which includes UWE) were from BAME backgrounds (Equality Challenge Unit 2014, pp. 210–211). Moreover, research by Boliver (2013, 2016), which confirms the findings of Modood and colleagues (Modood 2012; Noden et al. 2014), notes that:

> Despite being more likely than their white British counterparts to enrol in higher education generally (Modood 2012), British students from Black Caribbean, Black African, Pakistani and Bangladeshi ethnic backgrounds continue to be strikingly under-represented in the UK's most prestigious universities. (Boliver 2016, p. 247)

Boliver found that:

> when university applicants from Black and other ethnic minority backgrounds do apply to Oxford University or to Russell Group universities more generally, they are substantially less likely to be offered places than white applicants with comparable A-level qualifications. (Boliver 2016, p. 248)

Concern from the Office for Fair Access (OFFA) about discrimination and inequality in access resulted in a target set in October 2015 for a 20 %

increase in BAME students by 2020, while Conservative Prime Minister David Cameron decreed that from 2017 UCAS applications should be what he termed "name-blind" to tackle bias (Havergal 2015a).

Once in HE, there are considerable differences in BAME student attainment (HEFCE 2014) and subsequent progression into employment, compared with white students. In 2012–2013, a higher proportion of white students (73.8 %) achieved the highest grades of a first or a 2:1 compared with 57 % of BAME students, a gap of 16.8 %. In contrast, a higher proportion of BAME students (42.9 %) was awarded the lower grades of 2:2, a third or a pass compared with 26.8 % of white qualifiers (Equality Challenge Unit 2014, pp. 136, 140). Similar gaps persisted in 2013–2014 (Havergal 2015b).

This of course has an impact on students' chances of moving on to graduate careers in a highly competitive labour market as well as their chances of progressing to postgraduate study. Data on destinations six months after completion, also published by the Equality Challenge Unit, highlight disparities between white and BAME students on moving into work. Just over half of BAME graduates (51 %) were in full-time work, compared with 59.1 % of white leavers, while 10.8 % of BAME graduates were unemployed six months after qualifying, compared with 5.2 % of white leavers. Of those in employment, 40.3 % of BAME graduates were in professional full-time work, compared with 47.3 % of their white counterparts. So not only did fewer BAME graduates continue to full-time work, but fewer of those in full-time work were in professional roles. The Destination of Leavers from HE (DeLHE) survey found that three years on from the initial survey date of six months, the gap between levels of employment had widened to 13.2 %, with considerable differences amongst graduates from different backgrounds. Those from a Black African background had the lowest levels of professional employment at 65.9 %, compared with 78.7 % for white graduates, while those from an Indian background were the most successful in gaining graduate jobs at 79.1 % (Havergal 2015c; see also Rafferty 2012). Previous research therefore indicates that BAME students are under-represented at prestigious universities; as a whole, they are awarded lower grades than their white counterparts; and their progression to employment and further study suggests disadvantages compared to white graduates, though there are differences amongst students from different BAME backgrounds.

Alongside the above findings that raise concerns about disparities between white students and those from different Black, Asian and Minority

Ethnic backgrounds, a number of researchers have turned their attention to what factors contribute to enabling BAME students to *succeed*. Modood and colleagues, whose research has focused on students of Pakistani origin, identify what they call ethnic capital amongst South Asian communities in England (Shah et al. 2010; Modood 2012). This involves the transmission of aspirations, attitudes, and norms reinforcement, through adult-child relationships in families. They suggest that for middle-class British Pakistani families in particular, ethnic capital encourages successful participation in HE. However, ethnic capital may not ameliorate social class disadvantage, and they trace the interplay of ethnicity with social class as well as gender, that produces differences between and within working-class Pakistani families.

In the USA, research such as that by Yosso (2006) has also looked to alternative forms of capital as a means by which students from different BAME communities negotiate education. Yosso identifies a number of 'capitals', which include aspirational, navigational, social, linguistic, familial and resistant, which she defines as forms of community cultural wealth. While Yosso sees these cultural assets as a basis for changing and not simply fitting in to current educational structures, the notion of community cultural capital/wealth has been used by a number of researchers to investigate the factors that may enable BAME students to make successful transitions to HE (e.g. Leibowitz 2009; Liou et al. 2009; Luna and Martinez 2013; Wilkie 2014).

These studies challenge deficit constructions of BAME communities, by identifying alternative forms of capital used by members of these communities. Such capitals may act as means to counter the social closure of an HE field that is seen as dominated by whiteness (Bhopal and Danaher 2013) and middle-classness (Roberts 2010); family and community resources can be mobilized in order to compensate for the ways in which individual access to economic, social and cultural capitals can limit educational futures. However, as Modood (2012) and colleagues (Shah et al. 2010) emphasize, structural constraints, selective school systems and racialized labour markets, continue to influence the effectiveness of 'ethnic capital' in promoting educational achievement and social mobility.

For other researchers, it is young people's own agency that is important, rather than the specific interventions of their families and communities. Bagguley and Hussain's research (2016), focusing on British South Asian women, proposes that these women have developed skills of cultural navigation, which enable them to negotiate between different ethnic worlds and also different class worlds. Participation in HE is crucial here, allowing some freedom from family control and opening expanded horizons (Bhopal 2011). Bagguley and Hussain suggest that educational success is based on the capacity to resist rather than conform to family and community pressure and expectations around issues such as education, which subjects to study, marriage, and what career to follow. But they also propose that women's desire for occupational mobility for themselves is linked to collective ethnic identifications. Mobility is more than an individualized phenomenon, but is seen as a collective enterprise involving individuals' communities as well as their future families.

We now turn to the experience of students in the *Paired Peers* project. We firstly explore white students' awareness of 'race' as an issue at university. We then focus specifically on the BAME participants in the project. Seven of the students in the project were from BAME backgrounds, representing 10 % of the cohort of students that we followed through to the end of three years of undergraduate study. We consider how their experiences of getting in, getting on, and getting out of HE were inflected by negotiations around raced as well as classed identities.

The 'Whiteworld' of Higher Education

'Whiteness' theory suggests that 'whiteness is largely invisible to whites', it is simply the natural order of things (Owen 2007, p. 206; Rollock 2014), creating what Gillborn (2008, p. 162) has referred to as a 'whiteworld'. At university, the 'unspoken whiteness of the academy' can go unnoticed and uncommented upon (Clegg et al. 2003, pp. 163–164)—what Mirza (2006, p. 106) calls the 'normative whiteness' of HE. Certainly, many white students in our study did not notice 'race', though when asked, they acknowledged that in their experience, university is a taken-for-granted white space. The elite University of Bristol in particular was described as a white and middle-class world. Comments like those made by Sally and Liam at the beginning of the chapter were reiterated by other students:

> Most people are middle-class. Most people are white. So I don't think there's much of a mix. (Jackie, UoB, working-class, white)

> I'm in the ethnic majority. In [the University of] Bristol there definitely is a kind of white British majority. So that maybe made me feel like I fit in more. I think if you're in the minority you might feel differently. (Hannah, UoB, middle-class, white)

Like Liam earlier, Hannah recognized that she was a fish in water in the 'whiteworld' of university.

For some of the white students, who came from parts of England with an ethnically diverse population, particularly London, the lack of diversity they experienced was very different from home:

> Everyone here is very white and had quite a similar upbringing […]. I imagined it to be like my friends in London where it's a bit more multi-cultural and diverse. (Martin, UoB, middle-class, white)

> Compared to where I live back home it's just completely homogenous. […] Back home say, even just playing football on a Sunday, we've got like four different sort of groups. We've got like the Yardies or the Jamaicans, the Poles, the Sri Lankans, and then the Turks, you don't really get that at Bristol, it's more just white or Black. Like that's the thing […] you never really see many Black people in Bristol. […] And background wise, I'd say most people here were probably like the majority middle-class at least. (Luke, UoB, middle-class, white)

In contrast to Martin and Luke, Liam, who described himself as 'coming from an area of the country which is the least ethnically diverse', was surprised that the ethnic mix was so high, although this also reflects Liam's privileged middle-class background, which 'protected' him from contact with the minority groups in the city where his family lived.

Some students were aware that a taken-for-granted environment of whiteness and middle-classness could result in 'othering' and marginalizing of BAME and working-class students (Gillborn 2008; Vincent et al. 2013). Martin commented:

> Especially at Bristol, ethnicity is quite a key thing because not to be white is to be unique, and I think that does impact on how you fit in with the wider university population quite a lot. (Martin, UoB, middle-class, white)

He was therefore cautious about recommending the University of Bristol as a place to study:

> It is a really cool city and it is a good university, you definitely get a lot from your time here. But the reputation about Bristol is kind of true, that it's very representative of particular types of people, like not very diverse. So be aware of that. Even in the halls, it's still very…yeah, like white and middle-class. (Martin, UoB, middle-class, white)

However, there were other white students who did not see that the 'whiteness' of the HE environment might affect students from a BAME background:

> I think everyone's quite accepting. Because it is so diverse I don't think it matters, I don't think anyone of a certain background stands out negatively. If you're from a different culture I think everyone's accepting and there's something for each culture in university. (Jade, UoB, middle-class, white)

It was apparent in the ways in which some of these white students talked about 'race' and ethnicity that they benefited from what Levine-Rasky (2011, p. 247) calls 'a material and psychic distance from the entire issue of racialized inequality'. This distancing, she argues, allows 'evasiveness' about 'colour and power'. In contrast, for Black, Asian and Minority Ethnic students, going to university could mean a journey into the 'heart of whiteness' (Mirza 2006, p. 106), and we turn now to their experience.

Feeling the Weight of the Water: BAME Students' Experience of HE

Seven students from diverse ethnic and class backgrounds participated in the *Paired Peers* project (see Table 7.1). Four were from working-class backgrounds (three female and one male). The remaining three, all female, were from middle-class families. Their parents were of Nigerian, Black Caribbean, South Asian and Iraqi origin, and three of the students were from mixed heritage backgrounds—two had a white mother, and one had a white father. While all of the students were born and brought up in the UK, their Black and minority ethnic parents had all been born in their country of origin. All four working-class students lived in single-parent families with their mothers.

Whereas the white, middle-class students in our study could take for granted that they fitted readily into the university environment, comments from BAME students indicated that they were positioned not just in relation to their class origin, but also in relation to their ethnic heritage; they could feel the weight of the water (Bourdieu and Wacquant 1992) as Black and minority ethnic students. Three of them described experiences of being exotic others in a whiteworld. Nicole, a working-class mixed heritage Black student at the University of Bristol explained:

Table 7.1   Summary background information on BAME students in the *Paired Peers* project

Pseudonym	Social class	Ethnicity	Gender	University	Subject
Farrah	m/cl	Arabic Both parents from Iraq	F	UoB	psychology
Carly	m/cl	Black Both parents from Nigeria	F	UoB	Accounting and finance
Nicole	w/cl	Black mixed heritage Mother Black Caribbean Father white Parents separated	F	UoB	Sociology (transferred to theology)
Amina	Upper m/cl (Amina's designation)	South Asian Both parents from India (Muslim)	F	UWE	psychology
Adele	w/cl	Black mixed heritage Mother white Welsh Father from Jamaica Parents separated	F	UWE	History and international relations
Sariah	w/cl mother m/cl father	Black Both parents from Nigeria Parents do not live together	F	UWE	Sociology (transferred to sociology and film)
Shane	w/cl	South Asian mixed heritage Mother white English Father from Sri Lanka Parents separated	M	UWE	Economics, accounting and finance

It's so rare not to be white here.[...] Like my hair is always commented upon, and it's not a bad thing it's just...Like in the street, people will just be like 'Mel B' [...]. Or like random people just touch my hair [...] Or make comments, like someone called me Scary Spice the other day. (Nicole, UoB, working-class, mixed heritage Black)

Adele, a working-class student at UWE from a mixed heritage background, talked about her middle-class peers' fascination with her Jamaican background, which they found 'interesting and a bit cool and a bit exotic'. Her comments below chime with research into the white middle classes and secondary school choice by Reay et al. (2011), which found that middle-class families sought to extract value from their children's exposure to the cultural heritage of minority ethnic groups, although they were less keen for their children to engage with white working-class cultures and difference:

Adele: Thing is that I'm half Welsh and half Jamaican, people are very interested in the fact that I'm half Jamaican, that's really cool to be, I don't know why but it is really cool to be. There's a weird fascination with middle-class kind of left-wing people with Jamaica and Jamaican culture and Jamaican food. [...]

Interviewer: Can you give me a "for instance" for that?

Adele: They're always kind of like "Oh can you cook us some Jamaican food?" "No! I grew up in Wales, I have no idea." (Adele, UWE, working-class, mixed heritage Black)

Whereas Adele appeared to cope with being treated as an exotic creature, not least because it gave her a certain amount of cachet with middle-class students, Sariah, another working-class Black student at UWE, said that she felt 'uncomfortable' as a Black student:

I'm uncomfortable sometimes because I'm like "how come there's not many Black people?" On my campus there's not many Black people, and then on the modules that I do, there's hardly any Black people in the lecture or in the seminars. Bristol is really white dominated I would say. [...] It kind of makes me feel a bit uncomfortable sometimes when I'm the only Black girl. Like I'm not racist at all, like I accept people no matter what colour they are, but I think it's nice when there's a balance of different races and stuff in the class. (Sariah, UWE, working-class, Black)

While no students, BAME or white, referred to incidents of overt racism, there were examples from the BAME students of how they sought to accommodate occurrences of 'everyday' racism, involving what Vincent et al. (2013, p. 930) have described as 'mundane and deeply embedded, racialized assumptions and understandings that normalize and centre White individuals, and marginalize their Black counterparts.' Farrah, a middle-class student of Iraqi heritage at the University of Bristol, explained that she excused 'jokey racist abuse' from her friends at university:

I'll get jokey racist abuse from my friends, which to me is completely OK, I would never take offence at that. I believe things have become too PC [politically correct], people are taking things too far, they're scared of what to say. I think everyone needs to lighten up a bit. Like genuinely, I'm very proud of my background and everybody knows it, but I can also take a joke very well and play along with it. (Farrah, UoB, middle-class, Iraqi)

Yet having to tolerate such white racist norms allowed her white peers to remain unchallenged by the racist implications of their practices. Sariah explained how it was not just being one of very few Black students on her course that made her feel uncomfortable, but incidents such as the following:

Sariah: We were watching a film and they said "nigger" a lot. And she [the tutor] said it out loud. I felt so offended by it because, you know, that's what they used to call slaves back then, so I was really offended. And I was thinking "you can't just say the N Word".

Interviewer: And so your white teacher said that?

Sariah: Yeah. I felt like "oh that's really bad, you shouldn't say that". But if I was white and then I had a Black lecturer and they said, I don't know, what is an offensive thing about white people, and they said that out loud, if I was white I would feel really offended by that. So I don't think it's right that she said that. And I was going to answer her back and then I just said "do you know what, just leave it".

As Sariah voices strongly, in a contradictory situation, she, as a Black student, had to weigh up whether to challenge or tolerate the taken-for-granted racialized assumptions surrounding her. Both she and Farrah recognized that subtle (as well as not so subtle) acts of othering Black and Minority Ethnic people were simply part of 'how things are'. These sorts of incidents were not necessarily registered by white students, leaving them with the perception that racism was 'not an issue' at university, as suggested by Elliot below:

> Racism is very very rare. There isn't a great mix of people of different races, but I think that's more of a class thing, that it's a whole load of middle-class white people who come here. But there's no overt racism and within the student population it's not an issue. (Elliot, UoB, middle-class, white)

In this environment, the different ways in which students negotiated between their BAME identities and their HE identities generally involved processes of accommodation between family heritage norms and HE institutional norms that sometimes resulted in conflict. Their experiences did not all follow the same pattern, a reminder of the complex and differing ways in which intersections of class and 'race' play out in practice.

Five of the students in our study found ways to accommodate their Black or minority ethnic family background and the institutional and social cultures of HE. This included consciously acknowledging and negotiating issues of race (Nicole), but also appearing to ignore their ethnic heritage (Shane). Two of the students described considerable conflict in negotiating their identities as BAME students, as they moved into and through HE. Adele, a mixed heritage Black student from Wales, spent a lot of time at university embracing her Black identity, having been brought up by her white mother, while Amina, an Asian student from an Indian Muslim background, completely rejected her ethnic and religious heritage, and fought against the expectations she associated with it throughout her time at university.

In what follows, we focus particularly on the narratives of Amina, Nicole and Adele. Their experiences reveal the complexities of intersections of class and 'race' and how they play out in different ways, particularly at a time of transition and change. As Levine-Rasky (2011, p. 242) comments: 'who one "is" is not static, it is wholly relational to others, to culture and to organizations in which one moves'. Levine-Rasky emphasizes the complex interplay between ethnicity and class, so that intersectionality may be reinforcing or contradictory in its effects. Thus, as with Amina's experience below, 'middle-classness does not guarantee access to class privilege for ethnicized or racialized women.' (Levine-Rasky 2011, p. 241). Moreover, as Adele's narrative of her emerging Black identity demonstrates, being defined as Black may be an assigned rather than a chosen category of identification that positions individuals in relation to a white majority (Song and Aspinall 2012).

Negotiating HE: Narratives of Class and 'Race'

Contradiction and Conflict: Resisting Family Norms

Coming from a middle-class Black, Asian or Minority Ethnic background can provide resources, including family experience of participation in HE, that help with the transition to HE. For all three middle-class BAME students in the *Paired Peers* project, going to university was a strong family expectation, seen as an important step in securing a successful middle-class career, in the sorts of professions already established as part of their family tradition, such as accountancy, law or medicine.

However, while two of the students were happy to follow family tradition, (Farrah, UoB, psychology, middle-class Iraqi; Carly, UoB, accounting and finance, middle-class Nigerian), Amina's transition to HE to study psychology at UWE was a time of conflict with family expectations. Amina was from a middle-class Indian Muslim background. She made it clear from the outset that a place at UWE was a fallback choice for her. She gained her place at UWE through UCAS extra. UCAS extra is a service that allows students who have not received any offers for a university place (or have declined the offers they have received), to apply for a place on a course which still has places available. It operates prior to "Clearing", which opens after students have received their examination results, for those who have failed to gain a place at university.

Amina perceived herself as someone who should have gone to an elite university such as the University of Bristol. Her family was well off financially, and also had a long history of participation in HE. Her grandparents went to university, as did her father, her mother and members of her wider family (including three aunts as well as her uncle and cousin). Amina said that her father's heart '*was set on me being a doctor*', and until her final years at school, they had got on really well:

> I was really, really close to him in high school, like absolutely close to him. It was a really good father/daughter relationship. But as soon as I got into

the whole puberty phase and like the boys and the alcohol and stuff like that, that's when things went a bit downhill, he just wanted me to do well at my studies.

When her grades at school dropped, her father offered to send her to medical school in Asia. Amina refused, and said she wanted to stay in Bristol with her boyfriend and friends.

By the time she moved to university, she and her father were not speaking to each other. However, as her perception of UWE suggests, she faced considerable contradictions in negotiating between her chosen identity and her middle-class Indian Muslim family background. Moreover, neither gave her the basis for knowing what to expect when she moved on to HE, for although her family background was rich in experience of HE, no one had studied in England. She commented about starting university:

> I never really had a view of student life. No-one in my family before had gone to university here in Britain, I didn't know what I was in for really. All I knew about was freshers' week, that's all I knew, and that's what I was looking forward to.

The contradictions Amina experienced between family norms and expectations and her chosen identity continued throughout university. She was torn between wanting the things her father wanted for her—successful study, progression to a respected career in medicine—and wanting to dissociate herself from Indian Muslim values that she rejected:

> I'm not comfortable with my family's religious values and my family's cultural values. There are some parts that I take pride in, and those are the parts that I pick up and instil in myself, but there are some that I don't really want to take with me into the future and pass on to my children.

Yet equally, she did not like what she saw as the excessive socializing, and the lack of commitment to study, that she said were common amongst her peers at university. Like some other upper middle-class 'fish out of water' that we discussed in Chapter 5, who also had a critical view of UWE student culture, she perceived this as not matching the expectations and practices of her own class background:

> People are coming here for the social experience. I do that as well but I'm kind of here to study if you know what I mean. Because at first people are

very like "oh let's go and get drunk", whereas I'm looking two or three years ahead at where I would be from now, so I'm just trying to do as much as I can.

As a middle-class student, whose family had instilled in her the value of succeeding through education, she sought to stand out from others by aiming for a 1st class degree, and enhancing her CV through a range of extra-curricular activities—membership of societies, involvement in the university's peer-assisted learning scheme, working as a student ambassador, volunteering at a hospital, as well as an internship with Bristol City Council.

But she remained unable to repair the broken relations with her father, and as she came to the end of her degree, said:

> Maybe after I've got my degree and graduated it will show that I've actually achieved something and made something useful of my life, on my own. So that might change his perception.

In contrast to Bagguley and Hussain's (2016) research, which finds possibilities in South Asian women's agency and skills in cultural navigation, enabling them to move between positionings, Amina's narrative shows up the contradictions facing young women from BAME backgrounds in trying to navigate between different ethnic and class worlds, highlighted in McRobbie's notion of 'top girls' (2007, 2009). In order to become 'top' 'career girls' (McRobbie 2007, p. 718), McRobbie argues that 'ethnic minority women are encouraged to abandon multi-cultural difference and find ways of identifying with the majority' (McRobbie 2009, p. 42). Yet it is expected that they 'will also step forward as an exemplary Black or Asian young woman, on the basis of an enthusiasm for hard work and in pursuit of material reward.' (McRobbie 2007, p. 728) For Amina these contradictions created unresolvable tensions that continued throughout her undergraduate study.

Discovering a Black Identity and Negotiating 'Race' and Class in a Whiteworld

Adele was one of four working-class BAME students in our study, three of whom were from mixed heritage backgrounds, all with one parent who was white. Adele studied history and international relations at UWE, and said she was brought up 'like I was white' by a white mother. She only began to engage with her Black identity when she moved to HE. She explained:

> I have been raised like I was white and I was Welsh, and I realise I'm not. I still do class myself as Welsh, just mixed race. People from the outside ... the amount of times I've heard "what are you?" And I say "I'm Welsh." And they're like "no, actually what are you?" And I'm like "well my mum's Welsh and my dad's Jamaican". I always feel like I have to explain myself all the time.

On the one hand, Adele describes above how she was obliged to negotiate her 'otherness' in relation to white students. But she also saw university as her chance to get to know the Jamaican side of her family:

> My nan and my dad's family live in Bristol, and it was an opportunity for me to get to know them better. As I was growing up I would only see them maybe Christmas, birthdays [...] My mum always says "you were raised British" so I know nil about Jamaican history or anything like that.

It was Black members of her family who encouraged her to go to university. Her older sister challenged their white, working-class mother's views on HE, and encouraged Adele to apply:

> My sister was like "you're holding her back, she needs to go, she needs to do something". My mum was more "Why can't she just get a job?" and never really pushed me really.

Her Jamaican grandmother also supported her. Adele recounted: '*She was really happy that I chose to go to university so she gave me £500 towards uni.*'
While Adele was pleased that she progressed to HE, her otherness in what she experienced as a very white and middle-class setting, meant that it took three years for her to feel comfortable at university, and move beyond her initial sense that: '*Coming to uni is out of my comfort zone.*' In all her interviews over the three years, Adele was acutely aware of herself as 'other', and talked about negotiating her position as a mixed heritage, working-class student, which marked her experience of university. For example, when asked about whether she was a member of any university societies, she responded:

> That's one thing I wish. I'm not that confident to do that. I kind of wish I could get into something, maybe to do with sport, athletics, netball,

something like that […] I'd love to but I haven't got the confidence to join a society and do that. […] It's always in the back of my head "it's not for you".

In contrast to white, middle-class students who could simply continue with the extra-curricular activities that they had been involved in prior to university, Adele sensed that she might be out of place in a university sports society, a perception borne out by a comment from Francesca, a middle-class white student also at UWE. Francesca was an active participant in the university squash club, and she described the sports centre as well as the squash club as a white environment (even though the Elshorbagy brothers, world leading squash players from Egypt, were based at UWE at this time):

> Everyone in the squash club is white, and everyone I go out with is white. […] It's just interesting when you go into a law lecture and you see so many different types of people, so many religions and different cultural styles of dressing. And then you go to the sports centre and it's totally different.

An added barrier for Adele, as a working-class student, was that she had to hold a term-time job in order to support herself through university, leaving her little time to participate in additional extra-curricular activities. A turning point came at the end of her second year, when she successfully applied for an internship as a fundraiser for a charity. This was a paid internship, funded by a university-run scheme, which meant that she could afford to take up the opportunity. Not only could she gain new skills and enhance her CV, but her manager encouraged her to be positive about her capabilities:

> My job I think has helped me quite a bit […] Sometimes I have a meeting with someone and I say to my manager "oh I want to be like that". And she'll say "what do you mean?" I'm like "they just sit there and they're so kind of assured in themselves and you can see they're obviously extremely competent." But then she's like "they're about 20 years on Adele. Give yourself a chance, one day you will be like that".

While Adele faced considerable challenges as a Black, working-class student in a whiteworld, unlike Amina, these experiences had led her to develop new skills in cultural navigation. As she came to the end of her undergraduate studies, she expressed a sense of pride in her origins: '*I'm proud of it* [*being Jamaican*]. *I'm proud of being half Welsh as well.* […] *I'm very proud of both sides.*' And she emphasized what going to university had given her: '*Confidence. And a bit of sense of self-worth.*' Yet, as a working-class, mixed race student, these valuable gains were tempered with an awareness that as she progressed into the world of work, she did not have the family connections and economic capital that she had seen some of her white, middle-class counterparts making use of, in order to move on to a graduate career destination of choice:

> It's all about who you know. It depends what course you do as well, but a lot of the time it is about who you know. And if you are lucky enough to know people in the right places that can push you forward. So you can have a kind of advantage if your parents have the right connections. I'm just not really going to think about that, I'm just going to do my own thing and kind of try and get where I can, but there are some people that have an advantage, definitely. And I know for a fact if I don't find a job that I really want ... say by about September, I'm going to have to do a bar job, I'm going to have to do something so I can afford to pay my rent and things. Whereas some other people might be given a bit of time to maybe go travelling and to maybe think what they really want to do, and have a few trial and error things, but I can't, I haven't got the opportunity to muck up on too many occasions.

Thus, class disadvantages intersected with 'race', so that she was less likely than her white middle-class counterparts to move smoothly into graduate jobs. As McRobbie (2007) observes, achieving a successful graduate career requires possession of the social skills of confident self-presentation and ambition, but it is also necessary to have the means to transpose these into the workplace. This is not just a matter of individual capacities, but involves access to the capitals and resources that can make this possible.

Mobility as a Family Endeavour: Using Your Resources to Succeed

Like Adele, Nicole was from a Black, mixed heritage background. However, she lived with her Black Caribbean mother, who worked as a senior administrative officer in a school and who was determined for her daughter to do better for herself through education. Nicole described a family determination for mobility:

> [My mother] knew that she wanted me to do better than she had done. And my nan had wanted her to do better than what she had, and she bought her own house. I think everyone should work their way up one step.

Her mother used their membership of the Catholic Church in a highly strategic way to ensure that Nicole attended 'good' Catholic schools, at one stage changing the church they attended so that Nicole would get a place at a particular school. Nicole was aware how important this strategizing was:

> I think if I hadn't gone to the schools that I went to, I probably wouldn't have gone to university. Because my mum didn't really know anything about it. I think she would have wanted me to go but I think if none of my friends had gone... My cousin, she is 2 years older than me, I remember when she finished school—because of the school I went to it was the norm to go to university—so I was kind of like "oh are you going to apply for university?" And she was just like "oh why would you do that? What's the point?" (Nicole, UoB, working-class, mixed heritage Black)

Nicole then built on the opportunities opened up through school. In the sixth form, she found out about the Sutton Trust summer schools, which are designed to give students from non-privileged homes an insight into what it is like to study at a leading university (http://www.suttontrust.com/programmes/), and put herself forward. As a result of the summer school experience, she applied to the University of Bristol and was offered a place.

Her experience of being successful as a result of widening participation initiatives shaped considerable aspects of her university experience. She got paid work as a student ambassador on an Access to Bristol (university) scheme, as well as a job as a mentor in schools as part of the university's widening participation strategy. She also worked on the university's telethon campaign to get donations from alumni and, by her final year, was a senior caller responsible for supervising the shifts.

Her goals and ambitions also appeared to be influenced by the way that education had enabled her to be upwardly mobile:

> I think I want to work more within possibly teaching, just something that's not like in a big office, corporation kind of thing. I want to do something that helps someone, but that's so broad it could be anything. [...] I did a lot of shop work in the past, but I don't want to work in a shop for my job, so I think I might as well do stuff like widening participation type things ... possibly something to do with education, like closing the gap.

While this suggests that Nicole could simply build a successful university life and subsequent career by cultivating her special status as a student from a working-class, Black background at an elite university, she also needed paid employment in order to support herself through her studies. Her apparent success as described above, was achieved at a cost—she said that the first-class degree that she would have liked to aim for was not within her grasp given the time she had available to study alongside work. She also knew that she needed to gain experience through volunteering and internships in charities, if she wished to work in the third sector or in international development, which was her career goal, and she knew that her mother did not have any social networks that might open up opportunities for her. Yet she maintained a determined conviction that hard work would overcome the disadvantages that she may face compared with students from wealthy, middle-class backgrounds:

> I think obviously some people do have more advantages. Like I know one boy posted on Facebook yesterday about a job working for his brother who works in the diamond industry. He didn't even want that job, so presumably he's got a better job. So I guess in a sense people do have it easier. But like I said, if you work hard enough there are schemes out there, so there's no barrier. Like if you can get to university, I don't see the barrier of getting a job after.

This comment indicates the contradiction in her narrative, demonstrating how she both highlighted and denied the barriers she had faced and continued to face.

CONCLUDING COMMENTS: HE—A RACED AND CLASSED EXPERIENCE

Moving into HE is an important moment of opportunity for young undergraduates. Entering this new social space provides opportunities for change and transformation. However, students' capacities to position themselves successfully in the social field of HE are affected by the resources they are able to mobilize, and the raced as well as classed habitus that affects their sense of fit in the university environment. While statistics on ethnicity are important in providing an overview picture, they cannot portray how 'race' is actually experienced in real life social interactions (Aspinall and Song 2013). The experiences of the BAME students in our study provide an insight into how race and whiteness, as well as intersections of race and class, affect the experience of participation in HE. The taken-for-granted whiteworld of university described by some of the white students in the *Paired Peers* project, positioned students from other backgrounds as Black and Ethnic Minority, whether they chose to be defined in that way or not.

However, as demonstrated in this chapter, intersections of ethnicity and class play out in different ways for students from different class locations, and from different Black, Asian and Minority Ethnic backgrounds. Amina struggled with a desire to abandon her Indian Muslim heritage and to identify with the norms and practices of the white majority, whilst wanting at the same time to remain a high-attaining, middle-class young woman and achieve the high academic and professional goals that her Indian father hoped for her. Adele spent time 'discovering' her Black roots when she went to university, not least because she was confronted with being defined as Black in the eyes of white students. Although she became proud of her mixed Welsh and Caribbean identity by the end of her degree, she nevertheless knew that she lacked the economic and social capital of her middle-class counterparts, and this would make the transition to a desired graduate occupation more difficult. Nicole, a high-achieving mixed heritage student at the University of Bristol, came from an upwardly mobile working-class family. She was able to use the academic capital she had already accrued at school, which had partly been achieved by her mother's use of social capital within the church, to negotiate a successful HE identity, and to maximize her chances of success in her studies and, then, in transition to the labour market. Although this group of students is too small and ethnically diverse to allow generalizations, these narratives could be seen to represent three typical scenarios for BAME students from different class fractions.

The students' experience suggests on the one hand, that policy agendas promoting wise investment in education from successive Labour and Conservative-Liberal Democrat governments in the UK are proven to reap rewards. But the detailed accounts of young Black and Asian students' educational experiences in this chapter should also temper any premature optimism about success and social mobility. As McRobbie (2007) suggests, while some of those from privileged Asian and Black families may become part of the new competitive elite, alongside their white middle-class counterparts, those from lower middle-class and working-class backgrounds often remain unable to mobilize the sorts and levels of capital that are cultivated and used by the middle-classes, to ensure that they are able to maintain or improve their social position.

CHAPTER 8

Conclusions

Britain is still deeply elitist. [...] The opportunity to attend university—the elite institutions especially—and progress into a professional job is itself still too exclusive. (Social Mobility and Child Poverty Commission 2014, pp. v, 194)

INTRODUCTION

The title of this book describes the students who participated in our study as part of 'the degree generation'. We have described them in this way to highlight how participation in HE has come to be seen as crucial to attaining a successful adult life for young people in the early twenty-first century. We have shown how working-class and middle-class young people in the UK are affected by this expectation, albeit in different ways. For those from working-class backgrounds, participation in HE may involve considerable uncertainty, but it is now a *possible* future to be hoped for, while for middle-class students, HE participation has become not just an expectation, but a rite of passage in the transition to adult life. Nevertheless, uncertainty affects middle-class students as well. In a nation where it has become common-place for middle-class children to be made to enter into fierce competition and subjected to continual measurement of performance from a very early age, and where comparison to others is encouraged and institutionalized, 'Are we good enough?' is a question that haunts middle-class life (Sayer 2005). In this conclusion, we summarize the key findings of the study, address ways in which the inequalities we

© The Editor(s) (if applicable) and The Author(s) 2016
A.M. Bathmaker et al., *Higher Education, Social Class and Social Mobility*, DOI 10.1057/978-1-137-53481-1_8

found might be overcome or mitigated and reflect briefly on the politics surrounding HE and universities and their role in promoting or hindering social mobility in an increasingly divided society.

CLASS AND THE EXPERIENCE OF UNIVERSITY LIFE

As has been noted throughout this book, going to university is seen as a 'normal' part of the life course, of growing up, for most middle-class students. It is virtually taken for granted that they will attend university. It can be seen as a moratorium, a rite of passage, and a space for growing up and attaining independence for middle-class young people. As Lloyd, a middle-class student from UWE commented:

> I think it's always been expected that I'd go to uni, and I've never dreamed of not going—because that's too scary to start work and all that kind of stuff.

In contrast, students from disadvantaged backgrounds have needed to demonstrate more independence and resilience on top of all the other qualities expected from an undergraduate, in order to move success-fully into the HE field and find a place for themselves in the institutional habitus of universities, which are often imbued with a middle-class ethos. However, while we highlight working-class strengths we are not endors-ing the policy rhetoric around the need to develop personal qualities to mitigate against inequalities, rather, we show that these students are faced with greater challenges due to structural inequalities. The solution lies in challenging the structures rather than expecting more of individuals.

Schools and parents play a key role in assisting middle-class young peo-ple to play the game effectively, utilizing their knowledge of the system to maximize chances of entering high-ranking and elite universities. Private schools in particular have the resources to provide tailored support to their pupils in the application process. Thus, economic and dominant cultural capitals are deployed to secure middle-class young people places at top universities.

By contrast working-class students are what Reay et al. (2005, p. 113) call 'contingent choosers', whose decision to attend HE requires more consideration, effort and planning. In our study, working-class parents provided emotional support, but were often unable to offer specific help and information on how to get into university. State schools and FE colleges were less well equipped than private schools in preparing students for admission to HE. The resilience needed even to get to university is summarized in the following comment, made by Jasmine, a working-class student at UWE:

> I went to a very, very run down secondary school, it was basically the worst school in [my county]. But I sort of made the best of it, if you can in that situation. It was a very sort of rough ... well a lot of rough people who had had very hard upbringings [...]. But I sort of made the best of it and I came out with quite good GCSE results so I sort of put my head down and tried to get on with it, despite the distractions around me from other people who just didn't want to be there. People want to be here, you know, they don't just come here because they have to sort of thing, and do something they love as well, definitely, that's why I'm here.

As this comment shows, working-class young people have to work hard to get into HE. They are less likely to be surrounded by others planning to go on to university, than those who attend private schools or selective grammar schools, or simply come from the middle classes. They have to negotiate a sense of identity that is not always in line with school expectations (Mac an Ghaill 1988; Nash 2002; Willis 1981) and reconcile their working-class habitus within a middle-class field that does not recognize or value it (Ingram 2009, 2011; Ingram and Abrahams 2016), while the private school middle-class habitus imbues a sense of entitlement and superiority.

When young people arrive at university they face a transition which may be challenging for many of them: leaving the safety of home, coming to terms with a more independent style of teaching and learning, while taking the first steps towards adulthood and independent living. While many find the transition demanding, we have focused in Chapter 5 on the additional problems faced by working-class students in the middle-class environment of an elite university like UoB, leading some to feel like a fish out of water. Unlike middle-class students, they are in a minority, and can feel isolated and excluded, in a milieu that takes for granted knowing what participation in HE is all about. The economic constraints they face force many of them into term-time working, which in turn may exclude them from the extra-curricular activities that contribute to CV building. In the more socially and ethnically mixed environment of a post-1992 university such as UWE in our study, they are likely to find it easier to achieve a sense of fitting in, as suggested in the following reflection offered by Henry, a working-class student from UWE:

It's probably surpassed my expectations. Because I hadn't really any sort of friends that had been to uni before … [nor] my family, so didn't really know what to expect apart from like stuff on TV, which is a little bit more mental than what it is like. But it's been absolutely brilliant, time of my life sort of thing. Really, really good. Met loads of new people, I've got people that are probably friends for life now. […] So it's been fantastic. (Henry, UWE, working-class)

In this book, we have also drawn attention to the emotional disturbance experienced by some middle-class students, where the reputational affect of attending a less prestigious university is marked. The high level of knowledge about the hierarchical ordering of universities among students, reinforced by the way universities' reputations become embedded in institutional cultures, meant that attending UWE was associated with feelings of failure for some students.

Acquiring a degree could be seen as a process of *equalization*. As we saw in Chapter 6 the potential of working-class students in our study was realized and they achieved broadly similar degree results to middle-class students. For a time, the paths of working-class and middle-class students have run parallel and the distance in social space has narrowed. However, as they prepared to leave university and seek employment, there were signs of the gap widening again. Although all the participants had acquired high levels of academic capital, the financial exigencies of many of the working-class participants had inhibited their participation in extra-curricular activities and volunteering, which are becoming essential components of a CV that will suitably impress potential employers. They also could not afford to take up unpaid placements and internships, which are increasingly a major route into sought-after permanent positions. Unless they excelled sufficiently to get funding, they were likely to struggle to take on Masters level study, which is becoming the new basis for distinction under conditions of mass HE, providing a significant wage premium compared with Bachelor study alone (Lindley and Machin 2013). Thus, they were disadvantaged in terms of possessing lower levels of economic capital, and perhaps above all lower levels of social capital (such as the relative who knows a partner in a prestigious law firm), which are increasingly necessary to ease the path into graduate schemes and jobs. As became very apparent in our study: a degree is not enough.

It may be that the resilience and determination we found amongst participants in the study will carry them through to their desired future destinations but equality does not spring from an expectation that working-class people will draw upon personal strengths to defy a deficit system. As they prepared to leave HE, we can observe that the capitals which the middle-class students brought in with them from their family backgrounds and which helped them to 'get in', were still playing a role in 'getting out' and had been increased through the cultural and social activities attendant on their university life. Thus, we can state that the student experience remains one marked by class, which intersects with gender and 'race' as discussed in Chapters 6 and 7.

Our findings echo Stich's notion of class being omnipresent yet absent, with which we started Chapter 2. We have found it to 'manifest unabashedly' (Stich 2012, p.105) in university corridors, lecture theatres, seminar rooms and halls of residence. Despite its shameless presence in our study, in some ways it remained aloof and almost difficult to articulate. It raised its head in discussions of private and comprehensive schooling (Chapter 5), fitting in and belonging (Chapter 4), social capital and gaining employment, and whiteness and Othering (Chapter 7), but in ways in which those made to feel the negative valuing that comes with class prejudice felt obliged to bear it. As noted in Chapter 2, social class is not considered to be a legally protected characteristic under the UK's 2010 Equality Act, unlike gender, ethnicity and sexuality. Classism is therefore permitted to manifest in institutionalized forms without criticism. It materializes in reputational affect to create and maintain inequalities through subtle forms of class boundary drawing, which structure the perceived opportunities and limits of different universities in a hierarchically stratified field and mean that students at the two universities in our study led largely separate lives, consistent with a classed conceptualization of each university's milieu.

CONCERTED INTERVENTION, HYPERMOBILIZATION AND REPUTATIONAL AFFECT

While the working-class students in the *Paired Peers* project were successful in gaining access to and making their way through university study alongside their middle-class counterparts, our study also helps to extend understandings of how the HE experience continues to be saturated by class. We have proposed that middle-class families not only undertake concerted *cultivation* (Lareau 2003, 2011) to ensure that their children maintain their class position, but where necessary, they undertake concerted *intervention* to keep their children on track, or to get them back on track. These interventions go well beyond providing a supportive environment and taking an interest, but are informed by a knowledge of how to play the game, and involve micro-level involvement to mitigate setbacks in educational progress and progression. We have also shown how concerted cultivation in the family helps to develop habitus and dispositions in the young middle classes that involve mobilizing capitals to advantage, and in the twenty-first century, actively engaging in the *hyper-mobilization* of capitals to ensure advantage. Finally, we build on the work of Reay (1998, 2004, 2015) on habitus and institutional habitus, and Stich's (2012) work on reputational affect, to show the ways in which reputational positioning in a hierarchical and stratified field of HE creates *reputational affects* in both middle-class and working-class students. The strength of reputational affects is shown in our study not only in working-class students sensing how they are fish out of water in elite institutions, but in some middle-class students who see themselves as fish out of water in universities deemed to be less prestigious.

Consolidating Class Segregation Through the HE System

The classing of the student experience is paralleled by the classing of the HE system, as discussed in Chapter 3. Although the ending of the binary divide between universities and polytechnics created a unified HE system in the UK, the polarizing tendencies noted in other research (Bathmaker 2016; Gallacher 2006; Raffe and Croxford 2015), which have increasingly structured the UK HE sector into a three or four-tier system (Moodie 2009), are becoming consolidated rather than breaking down. There is a clear reputational difference between the Russell Group and the rest of HE provision, and many of the participants in our project were highly aware of the reputational positioning of different universities, even if they were not familiar with the formal groupings within the sector. Joanna, a middle-class student who studied at UWE explained:

> My mum was really upset about me going to UWE, because obviously Bristol Uni, for middle-class people, Bristol Uni is the only good … because it's like a red brick university and she wanted me to go there. But she's happy I'm at UWE now. I did look at Bristol University and she tried to push me to go there but I just didn't like the look of the courses as much.

And my sister's here and she's really happy, so I thought it wouldn't be too bad. (Joanna, UWE, middle-class)

It can be argued that while in the past, in the UK getting a first-class degree was taken as a marker of excellence, in the current socio-economic climate that has been replaced by attending a Russell Group university as a symbolically recognized 'guarantee' of quality. While there were always distinctions made between HEIs, the argument is that these are now more firmly embedded to create a tiered system: Russell Group for the elite, other universities for the mass, and college-based higher education and higher level apprenticeships as a third tier, likely to draw in mainly working-class recruits. A handful of non-elite applicants are allowed to filter through into the top tier, to maintain the impression of meritocratic selection. Thus, the class structure of dominant and dominated is recreated and legitimated through the HE system. Recently there have also been claims that Oxford and Cambridge Universities are actually qualitatively differentiated from the other Russell Group institutions, and, following Jones (2014) and Dorling (2014), the breeding ground of the 1 % who constitute the 'Establishment'.

In this way, it can be argued that the HE system, despite widening access, continues to be a vehicle of class reproduction. Ironically, despite this, in the UK context, all the political parties claim to be strongly in support of widening access and social mobility. A Green Paper published in 2015 by the UK's Conservative Government not only has 'social mobility' in its title, but has increasing access and success in HE participation for those from disadvantaged and under-represented groups as one of its key objectives:

> Higher education is an important driver of social mobility. As a One Nation Government, we believe that anyone with the talent and potential should be able to benefit from higher education. We will continue to push for better access, retention and progression for students from disadvantaged backgrounds and underrepresented groups. (BIS 2015, p. 13)

Critics might argue that such a vision and all the similar government statements that preceded it are based on a limited and meritocratic vision of social mobility: the opening of access to those deemed to have 'talent' is quite compatible with increasing social inequality. The talented can be rewarded exponentially more than those deemed 'untalented'. This, then can actually serve as legitimation for widening inequality, as powerfully described by Khan (2012), writing about schooling in the USA, in *Privilege; the Making of an Adolescent Elite at St Paul's School.* The idea of talent and excellence offers to those selected young people a sense of entitlement to the rewards that await them. Against this, we suggest there is a need for a different model of social mobility, an upward movement of all those confined to the lower strata of the class hierarchy, as arguably happened in the second half of the twentieth century in the decades after the Second World War. In other words, the social mobility of individuals must be accompanied by attacks on social inequality.

The pull of university is very strong, for both young people and their parents. While in the early and mid-twentieth century, as discussed in the first chapter, going to university was common for middle-class people, but quite a rarity for those from the working-class (Brown and Scase 1994), the expansion of HE, the ending of the binary divide between polytechnics and universities, government policies promoting widening participation along with efforts by schools to encourage pupils to 'Aim Higher' have all arguably combined to produce higher educational expectations across the class spectrum (Bradley 2015). Working-class families interviewed in Bristol for the *Ordinary Lives* project (Atkinson and Bradley 2013) all hoped that their children would have advantages denied to their generation, and they put their faith in graduate employment, perhaps because, in their day, a degree was more likely to secure a good job regardless of class background. Some students in our project grew up watching their parents struggle, and while they developed a sense of pride in their parents for providing for them against the odds, these young people, while not necessarily wanting to erode their class roots, strived for a life that was more financially secure. They spoke of the desire to escape from struggle and poverty, and to make something of their lives. They wanted to be socially mobile in terms of their own employment status. However, as they embarked on this road to mobility through educational achievement they encountered the hurdle of having to negotiate their way in a middle-class field.

As we saw in Chapters 4 and 5, this process sometimes entailed deep reflection on the value of their own capitals and a questioning of the value of the middle-class capitals it was assumed they wanted and needed to adopt. Indeed, the assumption that social mobility (or becoming middle-class culturally) is in itself something that all sections of the working classes require and desire is one that is problematic. Mobility often comes with a pull on the habitus causing uncomfortable negotiations about cultural value (Friedman 2015; Ingram 2011; Ingram and Abrahams 2016; Reay 2002, 2004). As we have seen throughout this book, the process of gaining higher educational qualifications can elicit painful emotions for some working-class people. However, gaining a degree is still desirable for increased opportunity. It is not possible to strive for a working-class job of the past, because secure working-class forms of employment do not exist in the same way they did and to strive for them is to look to a future of sporadic employment and low wages. In this context HE may become a necessity for the working classes in a precarious labour market context.

MITIGATING INEQUALITY: POLICIES FOR CHANGE

Sociologists have always been interested in both continuities and change. This concluding chapter has highlighted continuities which have emerged from our study: the stratification of higher education institutions (HEIs); the production of an elite from top flight universities; the difficulties working-class young people encounter in entering HE and getting the most out of the student experience; the social 'othering' that still exists within the student body. Although the culture and language that surround these phenomena may have altered towards themes of widening partic-ipation, democracy and inclusion since Brown and Scase wrote *Higher Education and Corporate Realities* over two decades ago, the underlying structures of inequality have proved remarkably persistent.

What, then, can we do to effect further or more fundamental change? Are there any possibilities for breaking these patterns of differentiation and disadvantage, apart from the efforts of individual members of the dominated classes pulling themselves upwards through determination and resilience, as highlighted in this book? While much of our book uncovers the continuing reproduction of inequalities in and through HE, we also seek to 'generate practical, actionable knowledge' (Edgerton and Roberts 2014, p. 193) based on this analysis. Here we consider just some of the actions which might begin to shake the structures of privilege, focusing on HEIs and their practices, the role of employers and on potential govern-ment policies.

The hierarchical system with a self-selected elite group of universities is itself part of the inequity problem, and focusing on entry to elite insti-tutions does not go far enough if inequalities are to be truly challenged. Nevertheless, if entry to UK Russell Group universities is the passport to good professional careers, then it is clear that these HEIs need to do more to recruit students from underprivileged backgrounds. Although WP policies look good on paper, the statistics show that little improvement is actually occurring in providing access to high-ranking institutions. Obviously existing policies need to be continued, but supplemented with more targeted policies. For example, HEIs might 'sponsor' low-achieving schools in their areas offering a number of scholarships exclusively for their pupils. To ensure that such students are not isolated and in danger of drop out, HEIs then need to ensure that adequate support is provided to integrate WP students into their departmental cultures. The DD lab project at Bristol's Graduate School (Timmis et al. 2014) has provided some pioneering research into this using digital technology which can be used to ensure, for example, that working-class students who have to work to finance their studies or take some time to travel into the university if they have to live at home to cut costs can still remain in touch with their tutors and access study materials; there is also potential here for linking such students together in virtual friendship groups.

The What Works project (Higgins 2015) has highlighted the importance of student engagement in ensuring retention and success. If students are to be engaged, it is important that academic lecturers and tutors, along with student support services, become more attuned to WP students' needs and concerns right from the start of their studies, moving beyond addressing 'deficits' in students, to making the practices of doing HE study more clearly visible and understandable. At a deeper level, this means challenging the institutional habitus of universities (Reay et al. 2005), which can be alien to those from working-class or BAME backgrounds. This would include more reflexivity and awareness of difference, and a preparedness to challenge taken-for-granted assumptions that existing customs and practices work best.

The high level of tuition fees and the erosion of financial support such as maintenance grants in the UK may not have deterred young people from applying for HE, but a lack of economic resources plays a significant part in expanding or limiting the student experience, and in preventing students from accessing a range of opportunities, including internships and voluntary activities, during their undergraduate study. Providing financial support for studying, that reflects the cost of living, does make a difference to students from low-income backgrounds, and is not mitigated by the replacement of maintenance grants with long-term loans. Internship schemes such as the one at UWE, that ensured students were paid when they were on placements, make participation in internships a possibility for low-income students as well as those who have greater financial resources.

'Hot knowledge' and family social capital were extensively used by middle-class students in our project to prepare for future employment. HE institutions in collaboration with employers could support working-class students to a much greater extent, by providing mentoring to final year students on job applications, by stopping the practice of unpaid internships, and by making more explicit the specific rules of the game of the employment sectors they wish to enter. Some employers have begun to introduce recruitment procedures, which deliberately hold back information on where applicants completed their degree when considering applications. This practice should be encouraged more widely. In addition, there is work to be done to get employers to value a range of experience that graduate applicants may offer, including part-time paid work while studying, rather than focusing mainly on the completion of high status internships.

'EDUCATION, EDUCATION, EDUCATION': THE POLITICS OF HIGHER EDUCATION

Education is about more than qualifications. Education is about us liberating our minds and liberating ourselves. (Jeremy Corbyn, speech at Scottish Conference of Unite, 15 January 2016)

In the opening chapter, we highlighted the fierce political debates surrounding UK government policy on HE. As we finish writing this book and while participants in the *Paired Peers* project are finding their feet in an increasingly competitive and precarious labour market, the arguments continue to rage. Tony Blair's famous dictat on his election as Prime Minister '*Education, Education, Education*' heralded his view that a highly skilled and educated workforce was a necessity as part of the 'knowledge economy' which Britain needed if it was to survive in a period of intense global competition. This lay behind the push for increasing the numbers going to university. But how was this to be paid for? Hence the shift in the burden of the cost of HE to the individual, through the introduction of student loans to pay for tuition fees.

The debate has taken a new turn with the Labour leader, Jeremy Corbyn, who was appointed at the end of 2015. He argues that education should be a right not a privilege and should be a lifelong experience available to all. Corbyn has stated that a future government led by him would abolish fees and restore student grants. In January 2016, Labour MPs sought to overturn the bill introduced by the Conservatives to get rid of the subsistence grants that had been available to students from low-income families. All this marked a departure from the neoliberal policy framework, which had been the consensus of both the major political parties in the UK over the past decades, that education was a benefit for the individual and therefore it should be the responsibility for individuals and their families to pay for it. In contrast, Corbyn's position posits education as a public good, benefitting the whole of society and which should be supported by state funding. As emphasized in Chapter 6, education is not merely about the acquisition of jobs, but about the broadening of horizons, 'liberating the mind' as Corbyn has put it.

The opposing stance was clearly displayed in the Conservative government's Green Paper of November 2015 (BIS 2015). While the rhetoric of the proposals focused on the desirability of social mobility and the need to ensure the provision of excellent teaching, the underlying neoliberal and capitalist principles were clear to see: HE should focus on the 'employability' of graduates and giving them the attributes and skills (whatever they might be) that corporate employers wanted. The instrumentalism of the Conservative approach to HE had already been signalled by the reallocation of responsibility for it from the Department of Education to the Department of Business, Innovation and Skills: HE should be a handmaiden to capitalism. Moreover, in line with the neoliberal version of capitalism the market should reign supreme: the not-so-hidden agenda of the proposals was to open up the sector much further to private for-profit providers, such as Capita who had already started to gain toeholds in the system; and through the Teaching Excellence Framework (TEF) to reward those providing the 'highest quality' teaching with the opportunity to charge higher tuition fees.

Such policies if adopted would have a clear negative effect on decision-making amongst working-class students, who would likely be driven by financial exigency to choose an HEI based on the cost of attendance. If, as is likely, the indicators of 'teaching excellence' (class of degree and employment outcomes and level of earnings have been mooted) turn out to favour the Russell Group universities like UoB, then the chances of obtaining a degree which is attractive to top employers would become even slimmer for WP students. Russell Group HEIs already benefit more than institutions such as UWE from the higher levels of funding they receive from the REF (Research Excellence Framework). It is not hard to see that the hierarchical stratification of universities would be strengthened rather than weakened by the joint frameworks of TEF and REF. Thus although the call in the 2015 Green Paper for a rebalancing of research activity is on the face of it progressive and in the interest of students, played out in the context of neoliberal capitalism such policies are likely only to deepen existing class disparities and perpetuate structures of elite formation described by Khan (2012), Jones (2014) and Dorling (2014). Whether Corbyn's alternative proposals of a return to a grant system is economically feasible may be in doubt, but it would certainly benefit low-income families. Otherwise what are the chances for upward mobility? This is the topic to which we now turn.

Moving on Up: Higher Education and Social Mobility

We stated at the start of this book that a key aim of the *Paired Peers* project was to explore whether HE was a vehicle for social mobility or a mechanism for reproducing the existing structures of inequalities. On the basis of our study, we argue that it can serve the purpose of class improvement for the working classes, but that this is more precarious than in the past. For middle-class students, a degree may offer a means of further upward mobility; however, what is increasingly apparent is that, for the middle classes, HE acts as an instrument of class maintenance, and a means of trying to prevent downward mobility. It seems, therefore, that the answer to our original question is that HE acts in both ways: as a vehicle for social mobility *and* a mechanism for reproducing the existing structures of inequalities.

We have been critical, here, of the meritocratic account of social mobility that seeks to identify individuals of talent from disadvantaged backgrounds and guide them into middle-class occupations and future lives. The problem with this account is twofold: it does not allow for the downward mobility of members of the dominant class. They can be force-fed to ensure that they still make it to the top or, in extremity, be rescued by the economic and social resources their families can muster for them, setting them up, for example, in entrepreneurial activities, or purchasing properties to provide them with a rental income. But, more importantly, this model of social mobility whereby individuals can thread pathways through the occupational structure does nothing to mitigate the pattern of increased class inequalities (Bradley 2016; Dorling 2014). The working-class as a whole remains immobilized. We therefore need policies to address the entrenched inequalities that inhere in a stratified system rather than simply seeking strategies to secure a few more places for working-class students at top universities.

Over the course of the twentieth century, there has clearly been a significant shift upwards of people from working-class origins into middle-class positions, fuelled by the expansion of forms of middle-class employment, the acquisition of higher levels of qualifications, with HE performing a vital role. Would further expansion under current conditions bring greater equality? Certainly not in and of itself, for participation in HE is no longer a straightforward passport to a middle-class job and lifestyle, but may lead to a life of precarity for many of its graduates, as predicted by Standing (2011). As Susan Robertson argues, the logic of global competition and the imperative of profit mean that only some entrants to HE will be selected for success and thus existing patterns of inequality will persist, with patterns of class, race and gender differences identified in this book underlying those processes of selection. Robertson states emphatically:

> An education system committed to social justice and not market justice would have a radical effect on politics. Only then might education become part of the solution and not the problem. (Robertson 2016, p. 22)

We agree. It will take major shifts in current policy and practice for young people, like the participants in our project, to have a fair chance to benefit fully from participation in HE, regardless of social or ethnic background. A fair and equitable system would not support university stratification, promote competition for funding, or allow for the elite to congregate en masse at particular institutions. If we are serious about ensuring social justice, then we need a comprehensive HE system, which does not hide behind the discourse of merit, to narrowly serve the needs of the privileged. In short, we need to reverse the processes of marketization which have taken hold of the HE sector in the UK and globally, and have a system that is both serious about fair access and also leads towards fair outcomes.

Appendix A: Family Background of Participants in the *Paired Peers* Project

Table A.1 University of Bristol middle-class students

Pseudonym	Mother's occupation	Mother HE	Father's occupation	Father HE
Adrian	Teacher		Chartered Surveyor	✓
Carly	Head of Programme Management	✓	Dental Consultant	✓
Cerys	Supply Teacher	✓	Minister	✓
Craig	Teacher	✓	Retired Steel Worker	✓
David	Secretary	✗	Accountant	✓
Edward	Artist	✓	Officer in Army	✗
Elliot	Housewife	✓	Film Maker	✓
Farrah	Pharmacist	✓	Businessman	✗
Grace	Social Worker	✓	Project Manager	✓
Hannah	General Practitioner	✓	Consultant Neurologist	✓
Harry	HR Director	✓	British Army (step-father)	✗
Jenifer	Teacher	✓	No response	
Lauren	School Teacher	✓	No response	
Liam	Teacher	✓	Chemist (Management)	✓
Luke	Learning Support	✓	Naval Architect	✓
Martha	Teacher	✓	IT Services (mother's husband)	✓
Martin	Homeopath	✓	Psychologist	✓
Max	Head of Year/Teacher of English	✓	Chemical Processing	✗

(*continued*)

© The Editor(s) (if applicable) and The Author(s) 2016
A.M. Bathmaker et al., *Higher Education, Social Class and Social Mobility*, DOI 10.1057/978-1-137-53481-1

Table A.1 (continued)

Pseudonym	Mother's occupation	Mother HE	Father's occupation	Father HE
Nathan	Doctor (General practitioner)	✓	Doctor (General Practitioner)	✓
Rose	Deputy Head Teacher	✓	Civil Servant	✓
Sally	Occupational Therapist	✓	Electrical Engineer (step-father)	✗
Scarlett	ICT Analyst	✓	Chartered Building Surveyor	✗
Sebastian	Teacher (ESL)	✓	Lawyer	✓

Table A.2   UWE Bristol middle-class students

Name	Mother's occupation	Mother HE	Father's occupation	Father HE
Amber	University Lecturer/Teacher	✗	Teacher	✓
Amina	Nursery Teacher	✓	Doctor	✓
Anthony	Teacher	✓	Personnel Manager	✓
Arthur	District Nurse	✗	Director of own company	✗
Christopher	Law Lecturer	✓	No response	
Donna	Part Time Sales Assistant	✓	IT Consultant/Programmer	✓
Dylan	Retired Managing Director	✓	Retired Vice President for large multi-national company	✗
Emma	Secondary School Teacher	✓	Business Manager	✗
Francesca	Social Worker	✓	University Professor	✓
Harriet	Administrator	✗	Head Teacher	✓
Jack	Teacher	✓	Teacher	✓
Jeff	Works for Scottish Health Services	✓	Retired	✓
Jessica	Accountant	✓	Self Employed Salesman	✗
Joanna	Barrister	✓	Tour Manager Music Band	✗
Joel	Managing Director of Business	✓	No response	
Lilly	Teacher	✓	Vicar	✓
Lloyd	Occupational Therapist	✓	Network Management	✓
Lynn	Secretary to Business	✓	Journalist, Business Owner	✓
Malcolm	Retired English Teacher	✓	No response	
Natasha	Head Teacher	✓	Architect	✓
Nicholas	Former Teacher	✓	Professor	✓
Oscar	English Teacher	✓	Artistic Director of Performance Art Company	✓

Table A.3 University of Bristol working-class students

Name	Mother's occupation	Mother HE	Father's occupation	Father HE
Amelia	Supermarket Worker	✗	Works Manager	✗
Anna	Accountant Clerk/Various Part Time Work	✗	No response	
Bianca	Lettings Agent/ Property Management	✗	Self Employed	✗
Claire	Midwife	✗	Yard Worker (Construction, Fixing Lorries etc.)	✗
Connie	Care Assistant	✓	No response	
Freya	School Office Secretary	✗	Heating Engineer	✗
Garry	Receptionist	✗	No response	
Harvey	CAD Operator for Met Police	✗	No response	
Jackie	Cleaner	✗	Engineer	✗
Jade	Local Council Worker— Land Charges Assistant	✗	Currently Unemployed (Lorry Driver)	✗
Justin	Secretary	✗	Window Cleaner	✗
Lizzie	Teaching Assistant	✗	Chauffeur	✗
Marcus	Pastoral Support Assistant	✗	PCI Services Manager	✗
Megan	Support Worker		Quality Manager	✗
Melissa	Nurse (step-mum)	✗	No response	
Nancy	Carer	✗	Civil Servant	✗
Nicole	School Secretary	✗	No regular employment (Nicole lives with her mother)	✓
Samantha	Housewife (Former Bank Cashier)	✗	Compliance Consultant	✗
Sean	Midwife	✗	No response	
Tony	Behavioural Support Officer	✗	Landscape Gardener	✗
Zoe	Works for Local Authority	Attending at start of project	Drives Machines	✗

Table A.4   UWE Bristol working-class students

Name	Mother's occupation	Mother HE	Father's occupation	Father HE
Aaron	Housewife (Former Accountant)	✗	Factory Worker	✗
Abigail	Admin/Gymnastics Coach	✗	Printer	✗
Adele	Sales Assistant	✗	No response	
Alfie	Nurse	✗	Engineer	✗
Ashley	Former Hair/Beauty/ Holistic Therapist	✗	Engineer	✗
Charlie	Civil Servant	✗	No response	
Gabrielle	Teaching Assistant	✗	Restaurant Owner	✗
Guy	Special Needs Carer	✗	No response	
Henry	Office Worker	✗	Scaffolder	✗
Holly	Sales Assistant	✗	No response	
Isaac	Secretary	✗	Manager at window manufacturing company	
Isabel	Lunch-time Supervisor/Learning Support Assistant	✗	Painter/Decorator/ Floor Layer	✗
Jasmine	Unemployed but runs holiday cottages	✗	Sound Engineer	✗
Keren	Cleaning Supervisor	✗	Manager for Tesco	✗
Kyle	Special Needs Teacher	✗	Truck Driver	✗
Leo	None	✗	Train Driver	✗
Miles	Cook	✗	Builder	✗
Rob	Nursing Auxiliary	✗	Agricultural Engineer	✗
Ruby	Childminder	✗	Van Driver	✗
Sariah	Hairdresser	✗	Policy work in law firm (overseas)	✓
Scott	Classroom Assistant	✗	Electrical Engineer	✗
Shane	Secretary	✗	Unspecified (Lives with his mother)	(✗)
Sophie	Clerical Worker	✗	Storeman	✗
Tracey	Teaching Assistant	✗	Property Developer (Step-father)	✗

APPENDIX B: MEASURES USED IN TABLES 3.1 AND 3.2

Metric	Definition	Source
1.1	% intake from state schools 2013/2014	Table 3.1a https://www.hesa.ac.uk/pis/urg
1.2	% intake from low participation areas (POLAR 3 quintiles 1 and 2) 2013/2014	Table 3.1a https://www.hesa.ac.uk/pis/urg
1.3	% intake from low social classes (NS-SEC 4–7) 2013/2014	Table 3.1a https://www.hesa.ac.uk/pis/urg
1.4	Mature (21 and over on entry) % full-time first degree students 2013/2014	https://www.hesa.ac.uk/pis/urg Table T2a
1.5	Part-time students as % all HE students	https://www.hesa.ac.uk Online tables
1.6	Continuation rate one year after entry 2012/2013 full-time undergraduates	Table 3.3b https://www.hesa.ac.uk/pis/noncon
1.7	% Full time Year 1 2013/2014 students from pre-university homes addresses within 10 miles	www.timeshighereducation.co.uk (accessed 27th July 2015)
1.8	% Full time Year 1 2013/2014 students from pre-university home addresses beyond 100 miles	www.timeshighereducation.co.uk (accessed 27th July 2015)
1.9	% undergraduates from beyond the EU 2013/2014	https://www.hesa.ac.uk Online tables
2.1	Postgraduates as % First degree students	https://www.hesa.ac.uk Online tables

(*continued*)

(continued)

Metric	Definition	Source
2.2	Research-only % of academic staff	
2.3	REF 2014 Grade Point Average per staff entered (GPA)	Times Higher Education 18th December 2014
2.4	REF 2014 Research intensity (GPA × % eligible staff entered)	Times Higher Education 1st January 2015
2.5	% Research in HEFCE grant 2015/2016	Times Higher Education 26th March 2015

Appendix C: Key Policy Recommendations from the *Paired Peers* Project (2010–2013)

- Social mobility is not just a question of gaining access to university. Universities need to support students throughout the student life cycle, including provision of help with CV building.
- Many young people whose families are just over the income threshold for extra financial support such as bursaries lack the material, social and cultural advantages of their more middle-class peers. Provision for these students who are 'caught between', including additional financial support, needs to be reviewed.
- Student accommodation may perpetuate segregation by social class, rather than provide opportunities for social mixing. If university is to broaden students' experience of social diversity, then universities need to consider mechanisms to encourage social mixing rather than segregation.
- While much effective provision for 'widening participation' students may best be integrated into good provision for all students, additional support to WP students through peer mentoring, particularly for first year students, would enable new students to learn from their second and third year counterparts.
- On courses oriented to particular professions (such as law or finance) students would benefit from a personal mentor early on in their program to help them navigate the terrain of preparing for and applying for internships and employment.
- Financial support is needed to enable students from low-income backgrounds to participate in extra-curricular activities and unpaid internships.

- Universities should properly target and monitor the schemes that aim to benefit 'widening participation' students to ensure they are not exploited by those from middle-class backgrounds who know better how to 'play the system'.
- There appears to be a bias towards careers in business and finance in university career fairs. More advice and guidance is needed for students who wish to pursue 'ethical careers' and careers in public service work.
- Career-planning and employability services should be alert to gendered patterns of decision-making about future lives and careers, and seek to encourage young women to aim higher, and young men to consider their future work/life balance.
- Post-graduate programs such as Masters are increasingly used by middle-class students as a means to 'stand out'. There is a need for provision of financial support for students from economically disadvantaged backgrounds to participate in these programs.
- The year *post*-graduation appears to be a significant period for finding employment. Provision of careers advice and guidance at this stage is crucial, particularly for those from disadvantaged socio-economic backgrounds. Where this is provided by universities, its effectiveness should be evaluated, and provision modified in the light of what can be learned.

REFERENCES

Abrahams, J., & Ingram, N. (2013). The chameleon habitus: Local students' negotiations of a multiple fields. *Sociological Review Online, 18*(4), 2. http://www.socresonline.org.uk/18/4/21.html

Adnett, N., McCaig, C., Slack, K., & Bowers-Brown, T. (2011). "Achieving transparency, consistency and fairness" in English HE admissions: Progress since Schwartz? *Higher Education Quarterly, 65*(1), 12–33.

Allen, K., Quinn, J., Hollingworth, S., & Rose, A. (2013). Becoming employable students and 'ideal' creative workers: Exclusion and inequality in higher education work placements. *British Journal of Sociology of Education, 34*(3), 431–452.

Archer, L. (2011). Constructing minority ethnic middle-class identity: An exploratory study with parents, pupils and young professionals. *Sociology, 45*(1), 134–151.

Archer, L., Hutchings, M., & Ross, A. (2003). *Higher education and social class: Issues of exclusion and inclusion.* London: RoutledgeFalmer.

Ashley, L., Duberley, J., Sommerlad, H., & Scholarios, D. (2015). *A qualitative evaluation of non-educational barriers to the elite professions.* London: Social Mobility and Child Poverty Commission. https://www.gov.uk/government/publications/non-educational-barriers-to-the-elite-professions-evaluation. Accessed July 2015.

Ashley, L., & Empson, L. (2013). Differentiation and discrimination: Understanding social class and social exclusion in leading law firms. *Human Relations, 66*(2), 219–244.

Aspinall, P., & Song, M. (2013). *Mixed race identities.* London: Palgrave Macmillan.

Atkinson, W., & Bradley, H. (2013). *Ordinary lives: Class reproduction and everyday practice in contemporary Britain.* ESRC Report.

Atkinson, W., & Rosenlund, L. (2014). *Mapping the British social space: Toward a Bourdieusian class scheme* (SPAIS Working Paper 02-14). University of Bristol. http://www.bristol.ac.uk/spais/research/workingpapers/

Bagguley, P., & Hussain, Y. (2016). Negotiating mobility: South Asian women and higher education. *Sociology, 50*(1), 43–59.

Ball, S. J., Maguire, M., & Macrae, S. (2000). *Choice, pathways and transitions post-16. New youth, new economies in the global city*. London and New York: Routledge and Falmer.

Bathmaker, A. M. (2015). Thinking with Bourdieu: Thinking after Bourdieu. Using 'field' to consider in/equalities in the changing field of English higher education. *Cambridge Journal of Education, 45*(1), 61–80.

Bathmaker, A. M. (2016). Higher education in further education: The challenges of providing a distinctive contribution that contributes to widening participation. *Research in Post-Compulsory Education, 21*(1–2), 20–32.

Bathmaker, A. M., Ingram, N., & Waller, R. (2013). Higher education, social class and the mobilisation of capitals: Knowing and playing the game. *British Journal of Sociology of Education*, Special Issue on Education and Social Mobility, *34*(5–6), 723–743.

Bathmaker, A. M., & Thomas, W. (2009). Positioning themselves: An exploration of the nature and meaning of transitions in the context of dual sector FE/HE institutions in England. *Journal of Further and Higher Education, 33*(2), 119–130.

Basit, T. N. (2013). Educational capital as a catalyst for upward social mobility amongst British Asians: A three-generational analysis. *British Educational Research Journal, 39*(4), 714–732.

Bhopal, K., & Danaher, P. (2013). *Identity and pedagogy in higher education: International comparisons*. London: Bloomsbury.

Bhopal, K. (2011). 'Education makes you have more say in how your life goes': British Indian women and support networks at university. *British Journal of Sociology of Education, 32*(3), 431–437.

Bohonnek, A., Camilleri, A. F., Griga, D., Mühleck, K., Miklavič, K., & Orr, D. (2010). Evolving diversity: An overview of equitable access to HE in Europe. *MENON Network*. http://www.Bohonnek.info

Boliver, V. (2011). Expansion, differentiation, and the persistence of social class inequalities in British higher education. *Higher Education, 61*(3), 229–242.

Boliver, V. (2013). How fair is access to more prestigious UK universities? *British Journal of Sociology, 64*(2), 344–364.

Boliver, V. (2016). Exploring ethnic inequalities in admission to Russell Group universities. *Sociology, 50*(2), 247–266.

Bourdieu, P. (1984 [1979]). *Distinction: A social critique of the judgement of taste* (R. Nice, Trans.). London: Routledge.

Bourdieu, P. (1985). The social space and the genesis of groups. *Theory and Society, 14*(6), 723–744.

Bourdieu, P. (1987). What makes a social class? On the theoretical and practical existence of groups. *Berkeley Journal of Sociology:A Critical Review, 32,* 1–17.

Bourdieu, P. (1990). *The logic of practice.* Cambridge: Polity.

Bourdieu, P. (1997). The forms of capital. In A. H. Halsey, H. Lauder, P. Brown, & A. Stuart Wells (Eds.), *Education: Culture, economy and society* (pp. 46–58). Oxford: Oxford University Press.

Bourdieu, P. (1998). *Practical reason.* Cambridge: Polity.

Bourdieu, P. (1999). The contradictions of inheritance. In P. Bourdieu et al. (Eds.), *Weight of the world: Social suffering in contemporary society* (pp. 517–551). Cambridge: Polity.

Bourdieu, P. (2000). *Pascalian meditations.* Stanford: Stanford University Press.

Bourdieu, P. (2002). Habitus. In J. Hillier & E. Rooksby (Eds.), *Habitus: A sense of place* (pp. 27–34). Aldershot: Ashgate.

Bourdieu, P., & Eagleton, T. (1992). Doxa and common life. *New Left Review, 191,* 111–121.

Bourdieu, P., & Wacquant, L. J. D. (Ed. & Trans.). (1992). *An invitation to reflexive sociology.* Cambridge: Polity.

Bradley, H. (2012). *Gender.* Cambridge: Polity.

Bradley, H. (2014). Class descriptors or class relations? Thoughts towards a critique of Savage et al. *Sociology, 48*(3), 429–436.

Bradley, H. (2015, April). *Aspirations and adaptations: Young people's careers in the context of neoliberal policies.* Paper presented at Journal of Youth Studies Conference, Copenhagen.

Bradley, H. (2016). *Fractured identities* (2nd ed.). Cambridge, UK: Polity.

Bradley, H., & Devadason, R. (2008). Fractured transitions: Young adults' pathways into contemporary labour markets. *Sociology, 42*(1), 119–136.

Bradley, H., & Hebson, G. (2000). Breaking the silence: The need to re-articulate class. *International Journal of Sociology and Social Policy, 19*(9–11), 178–203.

Bradley, H., & Ingram, N. (2012). Banking on the future: Choices, aspirations and economic hardship in working-class student experience. In W. Atkinson, S. Roberts, & M. Savage (Eds.), *Class inequalities in austerity Britain* (pp. 51–69). Basingstoke: Palgrave Macmillan.

Brah, A., & Phoenix, A. (2004). Ain't I a woman? Revisiting intersectionality. *Journal of International Women's Studies, 5*(3), 75–86.

Brake, M. (1980). *Sociology of youth culture and youth subcultures.* London: Routledge & Kegan Paul.

Britton, J., Shephard, N., & Vignoles, A. (2015). *Comparing sample survey measures of English earnings of graduates with administrative data during the Great Recession* (IFS Working Paper W15/28). London: Institute for Fiscal Studies. http://www.ifs.org.uk/uploads/publications/wps/WP201528.pdf; http://www.ifs.org.uk/publications/7998. Accessed Nov 2015.

Brown, P. (1987). *Schooling ordinary kids: inequality, unemployment and the new vocationalism.* London: Taristock.

Brown, P. (2003). *The opportunity trap: Education and employment in a global economy* (Paper No. 32). Cardiff: Cardiff University Working Paper Series.

Brown, P., & Hesketh, A. (2004). *The mismanagement of talent: Employability and jobs in the knowledge economy.* Oxford: Oxford University Press.

Brown, P., Hesketh, A., & Williams, S. (2003). Employability in a knowledge economy. *Journal of Education and Work, 16*(2), 107–126.

Brown, P., Lauder, H., & Ashton, D. (2011). *The global auction: The broken promises of education, jobs and incomes.* Oxford: Oxford University Press.

Brown, P., & Scase, R. (1994). *Higher education and corporate realities.* London: University College Press.

Brown, P. & Tarrock, S. (2009). Education Meritocracy and The Global War for Talent, *Journal of Education policy, 24*(4), 377–392.

Browne, L. (2010). As UK policy strives to make access to higher education easier for all, is discrimination in employment practice still apparent? *Journal of Vocational Education and Training, 62*(3), 313–326.

Burke, C. (2015). *Culture, capitals and graduate futures: Degrees of class.* London: Routledge.

Cabinet Office (2011). *Opening doors, breaking barriers: A strategy for social mobility.* London: Cabinet Office.

Carleton, D. (1984). *A university for Bristol: An informal history in text and pictures.* Bristol: University of Bristol Press.

Chowdry, H., Crawford, C., Dearden, L., Goodman, A., & Vignoles, A. (2010). *Widening participation in higher education: Analysis using linked administrative data.* London: Institute for Fiscal Studies.

Clare, J., & Jones, J. (2001, February 13). Blair: Comprehensives have failed. *The Telegraph.* http://www.telegraph.co.uk/news/uknews/1322418/Blair-comprehensives-ha ve-failed.html. Accessed Sept 2015.

Clark, B. R. (1978). Academic differentiation in national systems of higher education. *Comparative Education Review, 22*(2), 242–258.

Clegg, S., Parr, S., & Wan, S. (2003). Racialising discourses in higher education. *Teaching in Higher Education, 8*(2), 155–168.

Cook, A. C. G., Faulconbridge, J. R., & Muzio, D. (2012). London's legal elite: Recruitment through cultural capital and the reproduction of social exclusivity in City professional service fields. *Environment and Planning, 44*(7), 1744–1762.

Corbyn, J. (2016). Speech to Unite Scottish Policy Conference on 16 January 2016. http://www.press.labour.org.uk/post/137421807299/jeremy-corbyns-speech-to-unite-policy-conference. Accessed Jan 2016.

Crenshaw, K. (1989). Demarginalizing the intersection of race and sex: A black feminist critique of antidiscrimination doctrine, feminist theory and antiracist politics. *University of Chicago Legal Forum, 140*, 139–167. (Reprinted in D. Kairys, (Ed.) (1990) *The politics of law: A progressive critique*, (pp. 195–217), New York: Pantheon.)

Crenshaw, K. (1991). Mapping the margins: Intersectionality, identity politics, and violence against women of color. *Stanford Law Review, 43*(6), 1241–1299.

Crompton, R. (2008). *Class and stratification*. Cambridge, UK: Polity.

Croxford, L., & Raffe, D. (2015). The iron law of hierarchy? Institutional differentiation in UK higher education. *Studies in Higher Education, 40*(9), 1625–1640.

Crozier, G., & Reay, D. (2011). Capital accumulation: Working-class students learning how to learn in HE. *Teaching in Higher Education, 16*(2), 145–155.

Department for Business Innovation and Skills (BIS). (2010). *Securing a sustainable future for higher education: An independent review of higher education funding and student finance (the Browne Review)*. www.independent.gov.uk/browne-report. Accessed 15 Oct 2010.

Department for Business, Information and Skills (BIS) (2012). *Participation rates in higher education: Academic Years 2006/2007–2010/2011 (Provisional)*. London: Department for Business, Innovation and Skills.

Department for Business, Innovation and Skills (BIS). (2015). *Fulfilling our potential: Teaching excellence, social mobility and student choice, CM9141*. London: Department for Business, Innovation and Skills. https://www.gov.uk/government/consultations/higher-education-teaching-excellence-social-mobility-and-student-choice. Accessed Dec 2015.

Devine, F. (2004). *Class practices: How parents help their children get good jobs*. Cambridge: Cambridge University Press.

Docherty, T. (2011). *For the university: Democracy and the future of the institution*. London: Bloomsbury.

Dorling, D. (2014a). *Inequality and the 1%*. London: Verso.

Dorling, D. (2014b). Thinking about class. *Sociology, 48*(3), 452–462.

Dorling, D. (2015, February 12). Six trends in university admissions. *Times Higher Education*.

Edgerton, J. D., & Roberts, L. W. (2014). Cultural capital or habitus? Bourdieu and beyond in the explanation of enduring educational inequality. *Theory and Research in Education, 12*(2), 193–220.

Equality Challenge Unit. (2014). *Equality in higher education: Statistical report 2014*. London: Equality Challenge Unit. http://www.ecu.ac.uk/publications/equality-higher-education-statistical-report-2014/. Accessed 22 Apr 2015.

Evans, M. (2005). *Killing thinking: The death of the universities*. London: Continuum.

Fielding, T., Savage, M., Dickens, P., & Barlow, J. (1995). *Property, bureaucracy and culture: Middle-class formation in contemporary Britain*. London: Routledge.

Friedman, S. (2015). Habitus Clivé and the emotional imprint of social mobility. *Sociological Review* [online]. http://www.onlinelibrary.wiley.com/doi/10.1111/1467-954X.12280/abstract. Accessed 14 May 2015.

Friedman, S., Laurison, D., & Miles, A. (2015). Breaking the 'class' ceiling? Social mobility into Britain's elite occupations. *Sociological Review, 63*(2), 259–289.

Furlong, A., & Cartmel, F. (2007). *Young people and social change*. Buckingham: Open University Press.

Gallacher, J. (2006). Widening access or differentiation and stratification in higher education in Scotland. *Higher Education Quarterly, 60*(4), 349–369.

Gillborn, D. (2008). *Racism and education: Coincidence or conspiracy?* Abingdon: Routledge.

Goldthorpe, J., Llewellyn, C., & Payne, C. (1980). *Social mobility and class structure in modern Britain.* Oxford: Clarendon.

Havergal, C. (2015a, September 24). State-schooled are more likely to get a good degree. *Times Higher Education.*

Havergal, C. (2015b, September 24). UCAS: No bias against BME students. *Times Higher Education.*

Havergal, C. (2015c, October 8). Black graduates' job prospects worsen over time. *Times Higher Education.*

HEFCE (2014). *Differences in degree outcomes: Key findings.* Bristol: Higher Education Funding Council for England.

Higgins, S. (2015). *What works in raising attainment and closing the gap: Research evidence from the UK and abroad.* www.Educationendowmentfoundation.org. uk. Accessed Jan 2016.

Higher Education Statistics Agency (HESA). (2015). *Destinations of leavers from Higher Education Longitudinal Survey 2010/11.* https://www.hesa.ac.uk/ dlhelong1011_intro. Accessed Dec 2015.

Hoare, T., Bowerman, B., Croudace, C., & Waller, R. (2011). Widening participation Bristol-fashion: Embedding policy and practice at the universities of Bristol and the West of England. In L. Thomas & M. Tight (Eds.), *Institutional perspectives on Higher Education Research: Vol. 6: Institutional transformation to engage a diverse student body* (pp. 319–326). Bingley: Emerald.

Hodkinson, P., & Sparkes, A. C. (1997). Careership: A sociological theory of career decision making. *British Journal of Sociology of Education, 18*(1), 29–44.

Howker, E., & Malik, S. (2010). *Jilted generation: How Britain bankrupted its youth.* London: Icon Books.

Inglis, F. (2004). *Education and the good society.* Basingstoke: Palgrave Macmillan.

Ingram, N. (2009). Working-class boys, educational success and the misrecognition of working-class culture. *British Journal of Sociology of Education, 30*(4), 421–434.

Ingram, N. (2011). Within school and beyond the gate: The difficulties of being educationally successful and working-class. *Sociology, 45*(7), 287–302.

Ingram, N., & Abrahams, J. (2016). Stepping outside of oneself: How a cleft-habitus can lead to greater reflexivity through occupying "the third space". In J. Thatcher, N. Ingram, C. Burke, & J. Abraham (Eds.), *Bourdieu—The next generation: The development of Bourdieu's intellectual heritage in contemporary UK sociology* (pp. 140–156). Abingdon: Routledge.

Instructure. (2015). *Career preparedness and lifelong learning: A global perspective.* Canvas. https://www.canvaslms.com/lifelong_learning

Jivraj, S. (2012). *How has ethnic diversity grown 1991-2001-2011? Dynamics of diversity: Evidence from the 2011 census.* Centre on Dynamics of Ethnicity (CoDE), University of Manchester. http://www.ethnicity.ac.uk/medialibrary/ briefings/dynamicsofdiversity/how-has-ethnic-diversity-grown-1991-2001-2011.pdf. Accessed 27 July 2015.

Jones, O. (2011). *Chavs: The demonization of the working class.* London: Verso.

Jones, O. (2014). *The establishment: And how they get away with it.* Harmondsworth: Allen Lane.

Jones, S. (2013). "Ensure that you stand out from the crowd": A corpus-based analysis of personal statements according to applicants' school type. *Comparative Education Review*, Special Issue on Fair Access to Higher Education, *57*(3), 397–423.

Jonsson, J., Grusky, D., Di Carlo, M., Pollak, R., & Brinton, M. (2009). Microclassmobility: Social reproduction in four countries. *American Journal of Sociology, 114*, 977–1036.

Khan, S. R. (2012). *Privilege: The making of an Adolescent Elite at St Paul's School.* Princeton: Princeton University Press.

Lareau, A. (2002). Invisible inequality: Social class and childrearing in black and white families. *American Sociological Review, 67*(5), 747–776.

Lareau, A. (2003). *Unequal childhoods: Class, race and family life.* Berkeley: University of California Press.

Lareau, A. (2011 [2003]). *Unequal childhoods: Class, race, and family life* (2nd ed.). London: University of California Press.

Lareau, A., & Weininger, E. B. (2003). Cultural capital in educational research: A critical assessment. *Theory and Society, 32*(5–6), 567–606.

Lawler, S. (2008). *Identity: Sociological perspectives.* Cambridge, UK: Polity.

Lehmann, W. (2009). Becoming middle class: How working-class university students draw and transgress moral class boundaries. *Sociology, 43*(4), 631–647.

Lehmann, W. (2012). Working-class students, habitus, and the development of student roles: A Canadian case study. *British Journal of Sociology of Education, 33*(4), 527–546.

Lehmann, W. (2013). Habitus transformation and hidden injuries: Successful working-class university students. *Sociology of Education, 87*(1), 1–15.

Leibowitz, B. (2009). Towards a pedagogy of possibility: Teaching and learning from a 'social justice' perspective. In E. Blitzer (Ed.), *Higher education in South Africa: A scholarly look behind the scenes* (pp. 85–102). Stellenbosch: SUN MeDIA.

Levine-Rasky, C. (2011). Intersectionality theory applied to whiteness and middle-classness. *Social Identities: Journal for the Study of Race, Nation and Culture, 17*(2), 239–253.

Lindley, J., & Machin, S. (2013). *The postgraduate premium: Revisiting trends in social mobility and educational inequalities in Britain and America.* London: Sutton Trust. http://www.suttontrust.com/wp-content/uploads/2013/02/Postgraduate-Premium-Report.pdf. Accessed Dec 2015.

Liou, D. D., Antrop-Gonzalez, R., & Cooper, R. (2009). Unveiling the promise of community cultural wealth to sustaining Latina/o students' college-going information networks. *Educational Studies, 45*(6), 534–555.

Loveday, V. (2015). Working-class participation, middle-class aspiration? Value, upward mobility and symbolic indebtedness in higher education. *Sociological Review, 63*(3), 570–588.

Luna, N. A., & Martinez, M. (2013). A qualitative study using community cultural wealth to understand the educational experiences of Latino college students. *Journal of Praxis in Multicultural Education, 7*(1), 1–18 (Article No. 2).

Mac an Ghaill, M. (1988). *Young, gifted and black*. Milton Keynes: Open University Press.

Macmillan, L., Tyler, C., & Vignoles, A. (2015). Who gets the top jobs? The role of family background and networks in recent graduates' access to high-status professions. *Journal of Social Policy, 44*(4), 487–515.

Macmillan, L., & Vignoles, A. (2013). *Mapping the occupational destinations of new graduates: Research report*. London: Social Mobility and Child Poverty Commission. https://www.gov.uk/government/uploads/system/uploads/attachment_data/file/259380/Mapping_the_occupational_destinations_of_new_graduates_Final.pdf. Accessed April 2015.

Mason, P. (2012, July 1). The graduates of 2012 will survive only in the cracks in our economy. *The Guardian*.

Mayhew, K., Deer, C., & Dua, M. (2004). The move to mass higher education in the UK: Many questions and some answers. *Oxford Review of Education, 30*(1), 65–82.

McKenzie, L. (2015). *Getting by: Estates, class and culture in austerity Britain*. Bristol: Policy Press.

McKnight, A. (2015). *Downward mobility, opportunity hoarding and the glass floor*. London: Cabinet Office.

McRobbie, A. (2007). Top girls? *Cultural Studies, 21*(4–5), 718–737.

McRobbie, A. (2009). *The aftermath of feminism: Gender, culture and social change*. London: Sage.

Milburn, A. (2009). *Unleashing aspiration: The final report of the Panel on Fair Access to the Professions*. London: Cabinet Office.

Milburn, A. (2012). *Fair access to professional careers: A progress report by the Independent Reviewer on Social Mobility and Child Poverty*. London: Cabinet Office. http://www.cabinetoffice.gov.uk/sites/default/files/resources/IR_FairAccess_acc2.pdf. Accessed 20 Nov 2012.

Mills, C. W. (1956). *The power elite*. New York: Oxford University Press.

Mills, C. (2014). The Great British class fiasco: A comment on Savage et al. *Sociology, 48*(3), 437–444.

Mirza, H. S. (2006). Transcendence over diversity: Black women in the academy. *Policy Futures in Education, 4*(2), 101–113.

Modood, T. (2012). Capitals, ethnicity and higher education. In T. N. Basit & S. Tomlinson (Eds.), *Social inclusion and higher education* (pp. 17–40). Bristol: Policy Press.

Moodie, G. (2009). Four tiers. *Higher Education, 58*(3), 307–320.

Moodie, G., Wheelahan, A. L., Fredman, N., & Bexley, E. (2015). *Towards a new approach to mid-level qualifications*. Adelaide: NCVER. http://www.ncver. edu.au/publications/2784.html. Accessed July 2015.

Nash, R. (2002). The educated habitus, progress at school and real knowledge. *Interchange, 33*(1), 27–48.

Noden, P., Shiner, M., & Modood, T. (2014). University offer rates for candidates from different ethnic categories. *Oxford Review of Education, 40*(3), 349–369.

Northen, S. (2011). *What became of the bog-standard comprehensive?* http://www. theguardian.com/education/2011/feb/15/bog-standard-comprehensive-uniformity-specialism-faith. Accessed Oct 2015.

Office for Fair Access (OFFA). (2014). *Trends in young participation by student background and selectivity of institution*. Bristol: OFFA. www.offa.org.uk/publications. Accessed July 2015.

Office for National Statistics (ONS). (2012). *Ethnicity and national identity in England and Wales 2011*. http://www.ons.gov.uk/ons/rel/census/2011-census/key-statistics-for-local-authorities-in-england-and-wales/rpt-ethnicity. html. Accessed 28 July 2015.

Osborne, M., Gallacher, J., & Crossan, B. (Eds.) (2007). *Researching widening access to lifelong learning: Issues and approaches in international research*. Abingdon: Routledge.

Owen, D. S. (2007). Towards a critical theory of whiteness. *Philosophy & Social Criticism, 33*(2), 203–222.

Purcell, K., Elias, P., Atfield, G., Behle, H., Ellison, R., & Luchinskaya, D. (2013). *Transitions into employment, further study and other outcomes: The Futuretrack stage 4 report*. Manchester and Coventry: HECSU and Warwick Institute for Employment Research, University of Warwick. http://www2.warwick.ac.uk/fac/soc/ier/people/kpurcell/publications/. Accessed June 2014.

Puwar, N. (2004). *Space invaders: Race, gender and bodies out of place*. Oxford: Berg.

Raffe, D, & Croxford, L. (2015). How stable is the stratification of higher education in England and Scotland? *British Journal of Sociology of Education, 36*(2): 312–335.

Rafferty, A. (2012). Ethnic penalties in graduate level over-education, unemployment and wages: Evidence from Britain. *Work, Employment & Society, 26*(6), 987–1006.

Reay, D. (1998). 'Always knowing' and 'never being sure': Familial and institutional habituses and higher education choice. *Journal of Education Policy, 13*(4), 519–529.

Reay, D. (2000). A useful extension of Bourdieu's conceptual framework? Emotional capital as a way of understanding mothers' involvement in their children's education? *Sociological Review, 58*(4), 568–585.

Reay, D. (2001). Finding or losing yourself? Working-class relationships to education. *Journal of Education Policy, 16*(4), 333–346.

Reay, D. (2002). Shaun's story: Troubling discourses of white working-class masculinities. *Gender and Education, 14*(3), 221–234.

Reay, D. (2004). It's all becoming a habitus': Beyond the habitual use of habitus in educational research. *British Journal of Sociology of Education, 25*(4), 431–444.

Reay, D. (2008). Class out of place: The white middle classes and intersectionalities of class and "race" in urban state schooling in England. In L. Weis (Ed.), *The way class works* (pp. 87–99). New York: Routledge.

Reay, D. (2012). What would a socially just education system look like? Saving the minnows from the pike. *Journal of Education Policy, 27*(5), 587–599.

Reay, D. (2015). Habitus and the psychosocial: Bourdieu with feelings. *Cambridge Journal of Education, 45*(1), 9–23.

Reay, D., Crozier, G., & Clayton, J. (2009). Strangers in paradise: Working-class students in an elite university. *Sociology, 43*(6), 1103–1131.

Reay, D., Crozier, G., & Clayton, J. (2010). 'Fitting in' or 'standing out': Working-class students in UK higher education. *British Educational Research Journal, 36*(1), 107–124.

Reay, D., Crozier, G., & James, D. (2011). *White middle-class identities and urban schooling.* London: Palgrave Macmillan.

Reay, D., David, M. E., & Ball, S. (2005). *Degrees of choice: Social class, race and gender in higher education.* Stoke-on-Trent: Trentham Books.

Reeves, R., & Howard, K. (2013). *The glass floor: Education, downward mobility, and opportunity hoarding.* Center on Children and Families at Brookings. http://www.brookings.edu/~/media/research/files/papers/2013/11/glass-floor-downward-mobility-equality-opportunity-hoarding-reeves-howard/glass-floor-downward-mobility-equality-opportunity-hoarding-reeves-howard.pdf. Accessed Nov 2015.

Roberts, K. (1995). *Youth and employment in modern Britain.* Oxford: Oxford University Press.

Roberts, K. (2010). Expansion of higher education and the implications for demographic class formation in Britain. *21st Century Society, 5*(3), 215–228.

Roberts, K. (2011). *Class in contemporary Britain* (2nd ed.). London: Palgrave Macmillan.

Robertson, S. (2016). Piketty, capital and education: A solution to, or problem in, rising social inequalities. *British Journal of Sociology of Education, 37*(6). Special Issue on Piketty and Education. https://www.susanleerobertson.files.wordpress.com/2009/10/robertson-2015-piketty-education-solution-or-problem.pdf. Accessed Dec 2015.

Rollock, N. (2014). Race, class and 'the harmony of dispositions'. *Sociology, 48*(3), 445–451.

Rollock, N., Gillborn, D., Vincent, C., & Ball, S. (2015). *The colour of class: The educational strategies of the Black middle classes.* Abingdon and New York: Routledge.

Savage, M., Cunningham, N., Devine, F., Friedman, S., Laurison, D., McKenzie, L., et al. (2015). *Social class in the 21st century*. London: Penguin.

Savage, M., Devine, F., Cunningham, N., Taylor, M., Li, Y., Hjellbrekke, J., et al. (2013). A new model of social class? Findings from the BBC's Great British class survey experiment. *Sociology, 47*(2), 219–250.

Sayer, A. (2005). *The moral significance of class*. Cambridge: Cambridge University Press.

Scott, P. (2015, October 6). Roll up, roll up for the student 'experience'. *The Guardian*.

Shah, B., Dwyer, C., & Modood, T. (2010). Explaining educational achievement and career aspirations among young British Pakistanis: Mobilizing 'ethnic capital'? *Sociology, 44*(6), 1109–1127.

Shavit, Y., Arum, R., & Gamoran, A. (Eds.) (2007). *Stratification in higher education: A comparative study*. Stanford, CA: Stanford University Press.

Skeggs, B. (2015). Introduction: Stratification or exploitation, domination, dispossession and devaluation? *Sociological Review, 63*(2), 205–222.

Social Mobility and Child Poverty Commission (SMCP). (2014a). *Elitist Britain?* London: Cabinet Office. https://www.gov.uk/government/publications/elitist-britain. Accessed Sept 2015.

Social Mobility and Child Poverty Commission (SMCP). (2014b). *State of the nation 2014 report*. http://www.gov.uk/government/publications. Accessed July 2015.

Song, M., & Aspinall, P. (2012). Is racial mismatch a problem for young 'mixed race' people in Britain? The findings of qualitative research. *Ethnicities, 12*(6), 730–753.

Standing, G. (2011). *The precariat: The new dangerous class*. London: Bloomsbury.

Stich, A. (2012). *Access to inequality: Reconsidering class, knowledge, and capital in higher education*. Lanham: Lexington.

Swartz, D. (2008). Social closure in American elite higher education. *Theory and Society, 37*, 409–419.

Sweetman, P. (2003). Twenty-first century disease? Habitual reflexivity or the reflexive habitus. *Sociological Review, 51*(4), 528–549.

Teichler, U. (1988). *Changing patterns of the higher education system: The experience of three decades*. London: Jessica Kingsley.

Teichler, U. (2007). *Higher education systems: Conceptual frameworks, comparative perspectives, empirical findings*. Rotterdam and Taipei: Sense Publishers.

Teichler, U. (2008). Diversification? Trends and explanations of the shape and size of higher education. *Higher Education, 56*(3), 349–379.

The Res-sisters. (2016). 'I'm an early career feminist academic: Get me out of here?' Experiencing and resisting the neoliberal academy. In R. Thwaites & A. Godoy-Pressland (Eds.), *Feminist beginnings: Being an early career feminist academic in a changing academy*. Basingstoke: Palgrave Macmillan.

Tight, M. (1996). University typologies re-examined. *Higher Education Review, 29*(1), 57–77.

Timmis, S., Ching Yee, W., & Chereau, C. M. (2014). *Digital diversity, learning and belonging (DD-lab) overview and initial findings*. Graduate School of Education, University of Bristol. https://www.digitaldiversitylab.files.wordpress.com/2014/05/dd-lab-overview-and-initial-findings.pdf. Accessed Jan 2016.

Tomlinson, M. (2008). 'The degree is not enough': Students' perceptions of the role of higher education credentials for graduate work and employability. *British Journal of Sociology of Education, 29*(1), 49–61.

Trow, M. (1973). *Problems in the transition from elite to mass higher education.* Berkeley, CA: Carnegie Commission on Higher Education.

UCAS. (2014). *End of cycle report 2014*. Cheltenham: UCAS. https://www.ucas.com/sites/default/files/2014-end-of-cycle-report-dec-14.pdf. Accessed July 2015.

Van de Werfhorst, H. G., Sullivan, A., & Cheung, S. Y. (2003). Social class, ability and choice of subject in secondary and tertiary education in Britain. *British Educational Research Journal, 29*(1), 41–62.

Vignoles, A., & Crawford, C. (2010). Access, participation and diversity questions in relation to different forms of post-compulsory further and higher education: The importance of prior educational experiences. In M. David (Ed.), *Improving learning by widening participation in higher education* (pp. 47–61). London: Routledge.

Vincent, C., Ball, S., Rollock, N., & Gillborn, D. (2013). Three generations of racism: Black middle-class children and schooling. *British Journal of Sociology of Education, 34*(5–6), 929–946.

Vryonides, M. (2007). Social and cultural capital in educational research: Issues of operationalisation and measurement. *British Educational Research Journal, 33*(6), 867–885.

Wakeling, P., & Savage, M. (2015). Entry to elite positions and the stratification of higher education in Britain. *Sociological Review, 63*(2), 290–320.

Walker, I., & Zhu, Y. (2013). *The impact of university degrees on the lifecycle of earnings: Some further analysis* (BIS Research Paper No. 112). London: Department for Business, Innovation and Skills.

Wallace, D. O. (2016). Re-interpreting Bourdieu, belonging and black identities: Exploring 'black' cultural capital among black Caribbean youth in London. In J. Thatcher, N. Ingram, C. Burke, & J. Abraham (Eds.), *Bourdieu—The next generation: The development of Bourdieu's intellectual heritage in contemporary UK sociology* (pp. 37–54). Abingdon: Routledge.

Waller, R. (2011). The sociology of education. In B. Dufour & W. Curtis (Eds.), *Studying education: Key disciplines in education studies* (pp. 106–131). Maidenhead: Open University Press.

Waller, R., Holford, J., Jarvis, P., Milana, M., & Webb, S. (2014). Widening participation, social mobility and the role of universities in a globalized world. *International Journal of Lifelong Education, 33*(6), 701–704.

Wallop, H. (2013, September 27). Sailing is never going to float Ed Miliband's boat. *The Telegraph.* http://www.telegraph.co.uk/sport/othersports/sailing/ben-ainslie/10339551/Sailing-is-never-going-to-float-Ed-Milibands-boat.html. Accessed 15 Dec 2015.

Ward, L., & Shaw, C. (2014). University education: At £9,000 per year, parents begin to question its value. *The Guardian,* 26 February 2014. Accessed December 2015, from http://www.theguardian.com/education/2014/feb/26/university-education-parents-question-value

Warmington, P. (2014). *Black British intellectuals and education: Multiculturalism's hidden history.* London: Routledge.

Weininger, E. B. (2002). Pierre Bourdieu on social class and symbolic violence. In E. O. Wright (Ed.), *Alternative foundations of class analysis* (pp. 119–171). https://www.ssc.wisc.edu/~wright/Soc929.pdf. Accessed Oct 2015.

Wilkie, M. (2014). TeTimata: The first step to Maori succeeding in higher education. In H. T. Frierson, F. Cram, H. Phillips, P. Sauni, & C. Tuagala (Eds.), *Maori and Pasifika higher education horizons* (pp. 61–82). Bingley: Emerald.

Willetts, D. (2010). *The Pinch: How the baby boomers took their children's future and why they should give it back.* London: Atlantic Books.

Willetts, D. (2014). *Contribution of UK universities to national and economic growth.* Speech by Universities and Science Minister David Willetts to the Universities UK (UUK) conference. https://www.gov.uk/government/speeches/contribution-of-uk-universities-to-national-and-local-economic-growth. Accessed Nov 2015.

Willis, P. (1981 [1977]). *Learning to labour. How working class kids get working class jobs.* New York: Columbia University Press.

Woodman, D., & Wyn, J. (2015). *Youth and generation.* London: Sage.

Yosso, T. J. (2006). Whose culture has capital? A critical race theory discussion of community cultural wealth. In A. D. Dixson & C. K. Rousseau (Eds.), *Critical race theory in education: All god's children got a song* (pp. 167–190). Abingdon: Routledge.

Zimdars, A., Sullivan, A., & Heath, A. (2009). Elite higher education admissions in the Arts and Sciences: Is cultural capital the key? *Sociology, 43*(4), 648–666.

INDEX

© The Editor(s) (if applicable) and The Author(s) 2016
A.M. Bathmaker et al., *Higher Education, Social Class and Social
Mobility*, DOI 10.1057/978-1-137-53481-1

Printed by Books on Demand, Germany

Printed by Books on Demand, Germany